Past Praise for Frank Thoms

For *Listening is Learning: Co d
21st Century Teachers* (Rowm

"The best way to learn is from others who have been there before you. This book is filled with the kind of wisdom available when veteran teachers and young teachers share ideas in conversation. It is an extraordinary collection of wise suggestions any teacher will want to inhale."
— Susan Page, author of *Why Talking is Not Enough*

"*Listening is Learning* offers all of us who strive to become better teachers, valuable insight, inspiration, and the reminder that teaching is a collaborative process. Frank Thoms' excellent book illustrates just how much we have to learn from the hard-earned wisdom of other teachers, and how the pursuit of teaching excellence never ends. A valuable book for anyone in the classroom."
— Dinty W. Moore, author of *Crafting the Personal Essay*

For *Exciting Classrooms: Practical Information to Ensure Student Success* (Roman & Littlefield, 2015)

"Chock full of practical ideas deployed with reverence for kids and good humor!"
— Sam Intrator, Professor of Education, Smith College, Head, Smith College Campus School

"I have very much appreciated Frank's book. It's so important, truly a labor of love, mindfulness, and attentive care. I hope it gets all the audience it deserves."
— Anne Wheelock, author of *Crossing the Tracks*

BEHIND THE RED VEIL

BEHIND THE RED VEIL

AN AMERICAN INSIDE GORBACHEV'S RUSSIA

FRANK THOMS

Published by SparkPress, a BookSparks imprint,
A division of SparkPoint Studio, LLC
Phoenix, Arizona, USA, 85007
www.gosparkpress.com

Published 2020
Printed in the United States of America
ISBN: 978-1-68463-055-4 (pbk)
ISBN: 978-1-68463-056-1 (e-bk)
Library of Congress Control Number: 2020905897

Formatting by Kiran Spees

In loving memory of Elvira Nikolaevna Gnes,
Irina Nikolaevna Grigorieva,
and
Raisa Vladimirovna Murachik,
of Leningrad School Nº 185

"I thought it was 'If a body catch a body,'" I said. "Anyway, I keep picturing all these little kids playing some game in this big field of rye and all. Thousands of little kids, and nobody's around—nobody big, I mean—except me. And I'm standing on the edge of some crazy cliff. What I have to do, I have to catch everybody if they start to go over the cliff—I mean if they're running and they don't look where they're going I have to come out from somewhere and catch them. That's all I'd do all day. I'd just be the catcher in the rye and all. I know it's crazy, but that's the only thing I'd really like to be. I know it's crazy."

—J.D. Salinger, *The Catcher in the Rye*
(Boston: Little Brown and Company, 1951), 101

After school, Thoms will walk to his hotel room on the Nevsky Prospekt with a small tape recorder pressed against his cheek. He refuses to forget a smile, a tear, or an important confrontation with Soviet life. He gathers impressions of the Soviet Union like a real-life Holden Caulfield, the consummate social satirist. Nothing seems to escape his discerning eye. By watching and interacting, Thoms believes he is helping civilization from going over the cliff—a teacher in the rye.

—Keith Sharon, "'Teacher in the Rye' Works Wonders with Gum: NH Man Faces Sticky Problems in Soviet Schools,"
Manchester Union Leader, January 21, 1987

Bizarro by Wayno® and Piraro
copyright ©2018 Bizarro Studios

CONTENTS

INTRODUCTION

Russia is a riddle wrapped in a mystery inside an enigma.
Winston Churchill, radio broadcast, October 1939

I grew up in a world of mechanical toys with backs and bottoms and tiny metal tabs that invited prying. Some were wind-ups that whirred and buzzed in unpredictable directions. Others stood still, playing tin drums or running strings around pulleys. Most were made in Japan. I played with them, took them apart, and reassembled them.

Typewriters fascinated me, though I observed more than I actually typed. I tinkered with the open back of my black Remington Standard. When my finger pushed a circular metal-rimmed key, I watched its linked mechanical arm bring upper- and-lower-case letters to the paper on the black roller; its position determined which letter struck the paper. I tried a black-and-red ribbon and enjoyed the chance to choose a color.

I would peer through the narrow hardboard slits at the back of my Motorola table radio. I applied gentle pressure to the on-switch until it clicked to see the orange glow alight in vacuum tubes bringing in the sound. I was part of its creation.

The front had a dark-brown-glazed, plastic Venetian design; hidden openings let out the sound. Late at night, I would spin the right-hand knob, sliding its red-line dial at the top behind clear plastic. Stations having static slid by until I came to WROW 590 AM in Albany or WTRY 980 AM in Troy, broadcasting from New York over the Taconic Ridge. No presets, nothing automatic, and no worries except Mom, who might discover my late-night listening to *The Inner Sanctum* or *The Jack Benny Show*. The radio was mine and sat in its special place on the shelf by my pillow. And I discovered Radio Moscow, fascinated more by where it broadcasted from than with its content, which made little sense to me.

The Motorola was my private ticket to life beyond my family and the small inn where I grew up. *Mr. I. A. Moto, Japanese Investigator* let me taste Asian ingenuity; *The Inner Sanctum* scared the hell out of me; and Fibber Magee, Bob Hope, Fred Allen, and *Amos 'n' Andy* made me laugh and laugh.

Perhaps it was my childhood curiosity with mechanical things that provided tabs for my mind to pry beneath the obvious, particularly when it came to the secrets of Russian and Soviet history and culture.

I remember sitting in Miss Karasek's fourth-grade classroom staring at the *My Weekly Reader* wall chart showing the red Soviet Union spreading halfway around the world. Eleven time zones! Red, the only color on the chart. Less than five years later, the chart had expanded to include Mao's China, a red more etched in my mind. What would become of us? Would the red armies march beyond their borders? No wonder that, years later, American authorities feared a domino effect in Southeast Asia.

Later in that same classroom in my New England town, I read about Russia in *The Los Angeles Times*—why I had the paper, I don't remember. One article translated from a Russian publication cited two "Russian inventors": Thomas Edisonsky as the inventor of the light bulb, and Alexander Bellsky, the inventor of the telephone. That story stayed with me.

Who were these Soviets, these Communists? Why did we struggle with one another? Why did we compete? On October 4, 1957, my college roommate and I read in *The New York Times* about Sputnik, the beeping, beach-ball-sized, Soviet first satellite in space. Why them first? We were falling behind! Then a month later, Laika, a Soviet dog in orbit, another first! Four years later, Yuri Gagarin became the first man in space, ten months before John Glenn, the first American. Two years later, Valentina Tereshkova, the first woman, another Soviet first!

My junior year in college, I sat high up in a lecture hall taking notes for Professor R. G. L. Waite's enthralling lectures on Russia's tsars. His portrayal of their reigns, the Russian landscape, and the inner psyche of its people has never left me. I imagined some day that I would search out the Russian people. Years later as a new teacher, with the encouragement of my first mentor, I taught Marxist socialism, Russian history, and the Soviet Union to eighth-graders. For the next twenty years in my classroom, I pursued my curiosity of all things Russian and Soviet.

BY THE TIME Mikhail Gorbachev became General Secretary of the Communist Party of the Soviet Union in March 1985, I was tired of reading Soviet propaganda, its braggadocio to the rest of the world about its space spectaculars, military might, and expanding nuclear arsenal. And I disdained reading anti-Soviet chapters in textbooks and listening to US pundits take potshots at Russians.

When I first thought about traveling to the Soviet Union, I imagined going behind the Iron Curtain to find "real Russians." I wanted to meet the Russian people on their turf, listen to their joys and woes, discover who they were. I would look for common ground, to connect with them, not to judge but to learn, not to bring America to them, but to be an American with them.

Not long after I arrived, I realized that I needed to traverse another layer, what I've come to call the red veil: the face of Communism that the Soviet Union projected onto its citizens, foreign visitors, and the world at large. It was spearheaded by Intourist, Russia's official travel agency, which made arrangements for all incoming foreign groups. Foreigners were situated in international hotels (verboten to Soviets). Bilingual guides wearing headscarves organized and led excursions and herded tourists into special buses to official sites.

In Moscow, guides shepherded people to Red Square, the Kremlin, Lenin's Mausoleum, St. Basils, GUM (the largest Soviet department store), the Palace of Pioneers, and the Revolution Square and Mayakovskaya metro stations. In Leningrad, they visited the Hermitage and Winter Palace, Peterhof, Mariinsky Theatre, St. Issacs Cathedral, Peter & Paul Fortress, and Nevsky Prospekt (Avenue). Every Intourist tour included a stop at a Beryozka shop for foreigners only, where they could spend their currency on Soviet souvenirs.

Churchill's delineation of the Iron Curtain was an unintentional reflection of the historical Russian attitude—viewed from the Russian side of his curtain—that Russia was living in an armed camp. Despite its mammoth size, it had vulnerable borders. Russians believed they needed to be on constant alert for foreign invasion. The red veil would offer a layer of protection. With the arrival of Gorbachev and his openness to the West and implementing his policies of *glasnost* and *perestroika*, the Iron Curtain seemed less intimidating. Once I flew over it, I felt free to explore behind the red veil.

But why the red veil? Communism is synonymous with red. Red resides deep in Russian culture. The word for red is *krasni*, which means "beautiful." Red was integral to tsarist flags and banners. Vladimir Lenin's Bolshevik Red Army defeated the White Army to establish the Soviet Union. The Bolsheviks decreed red to represent the blood of its workers; designed a red flag, symbolized by its giant constant fluttering flag over the Kremlin; deployed red stars on banners and uniforms; required students to wear red-background Lenin pins and red Pioneer scarves; and incorporated Red Square for its parades and demonstrations.

For me, the Soviet red became implanted in my fourth-grade classroom with *My Weekly Reader* maps. Growing up during the Cold War, we referred to Soviets as "Reds" and often vocalized, "Better dead than red." And in teaching about the Russians and the Soviet Union for twenty-five years, red images would sometimes dominate the walls of my classroom. In the mid-eighties, I'd met Soviets coming to America. I decided then that I would travel to the Soviet Union to meet with Russians.

In October 1985, I took my first opportunity to be part of a tour group trip directed by Intourist, the Soviet travel agency. After this first trip, my best chance to return and explore deeply behind the red veil would be as a teacher. I set my sights on the US–Soviet Exchange Teacher program, the only avenue to teaching in a Soviet school. With persistence, I was able to secure not only one but two exchanges to schools Nº 185 and Nº 169, both in Leningrad; and during our holidays, I bonded on my own with school Nº 21 in Moscow. I taught children from seven to seventeen using Soviet English-language texts and my own materials.

In the summer of 1990, I served as a counselor at a three-nation international Pioneer camp in Alma-Ata, Kazakhstan. I returned the following January to teach at School Nº 15, where sixteen-year-olds cajoled me to ponder the afterlife and reincarnation. And three years after the fall of Communism, I traveled to Yekaterinburg in the new Russia to lead a seminar for teachers who would be coming to America. Eight trips, a year of my life.

A READER MIGHT ask: "How will learning about Russians from thirty years ago have any meaning for me today?" As an American, I came at a time when Soviets under Mikhail Gorbachev were opening up

to themselves and to the world. My Russian friends expressed their
thoughts and feelings to me about their lives, their country, and the
United States. I was privileged to gain their trust and be invited into
their confidence. I felt I'd come to know them.

It was a unique time in Soviet history in which Mikhail
Gorbachev was attempting to uproot Communist norms and create
a more open society, his effort lasting less than seven years. After the
collapse of Communism and his resignation on Christmas day, 1991,
the new Russia under Boris Yeltsin struggled with governmental rule
and economic reform. Within ten years Vladimir Putin was able to
form his own autocratic dynasty, returning to Russia's long tradition
of one-man rule originating from its first tsar, Ivan III, in the mid-fif-
teenth century.

This pivotal time under Gorbachev reminded me of America in
the sixties when the country's norms were challenged and repudiated
in hopes for a better society. Had a young Russian teacher come to
America in the sixties, his ventures would have been similar to mine
in the Soviet Union in the eighties. He might well have come away
thinking he understood Americans, as I had thought I understood
the Russians. And I, who was a teacher in the sixties, believe that
Americans remain much the same people we were then, allowing for
cultural changes. Hence my contention that Russians are Russians,
Soviet or not.

A friend asked me after I returned from my first trip, "Why
would you, Frank, who claim to be interested in understanding your
inner self, choose to do it in one of the most inaccessible countries
on the planet?" A baffling question. I intended to travel behind the
Iron Curtain to meet real Russians. I wasn't thinking about me. Yet
her question provoked me to realize I would have to reveal myself
to Russians if I expected them to do the same to me. Were I not to,
I would not have a chance to know them beyond external niceties.
Another way to say it: If I were to guard who I was, the Russians

would emulate that posture. I would have come home able to share only what I'd observed, not what I could have learned from the people. And since childhood, I had abhorred feeling outside. I had always wanted to belong—and to do that, I had to become vulnerable.

Behind the Red Veil: An American inside Gorbachev's Russia is a cultural memoir, accounts of my interactions with Russians, mostly through teaching in Soviet schools. I sought to uncover the spirit of a people who were emerging—temporarily as it was—from centuries of living under tsarist and Communist totalitarianism. As readers, you will travel alongside this American in his search to know himself as he sought to understand the lives of Russians in the last days of Soviet society: their customs, hopes, fears, revelations, heart, and soul.

I
AWAY FROM THE TOUR BUS

Standing before her "children," she revealed a curious intensity, directing them with attentive, quizzical, and scowling looks. She hadn't noticed me. She was internalizing a Soviet teacher's demeanor.

Young Pioneer, Moscow, Oct. '85

A brisk wind startles us as we step down the Aeroflot ramp and traverse the tarmac of Leningrad's Pulkovo II Airport in October 1985. A mist hovers below the night sky. Jet engines swallow the sounds of our voices as we slink toward a darkened terminal. We pass under blue flickering neon signs—Leningrad/Ленинград—and step through a half-opened, broken aluminum-framed doorway.

We are in a bleak space surrounded by unfamiliar sights and sounds. No sign of the Red Sox, no 7-Eleven, no colleagues. I've entered a cocoon spun by Intourist, the Soviet travel agency. My eighteen fellow travelers and I—the only foreigners in the airport—have agreed to abide by the tour's expectations.

But I'm longing to discover what I will not be invited to see.

At customs, I wait. I meet the cold glare of an *apparatchik* in his olive-green uniform beneath a dangling incandescent bulb. His leery eyes glare at me from under his cap. He snatches my passport and visa, scrutinizes them, glares again, pauses for what seems an eternity . . . Will he find fault with my papers? . . . He's taking a long time . . . I feel the cold. Is he going to turn me away? . . . *Thump! Thump! Thump!* He stamps my visa but not my passport. He returns both, minus the visa section that will let authorities know that I'm in his Soviet Union.

At security, another official X-rays my baggage, inspects my hand luggage. I withhold my film from the "Film-Safe" machine. He glares at me, then ruffles through my camera bag. Without looking he swirls his pen on my customs declaration and directs me to a dark corner where my group is assembling.

I'm on Russian soil. Breathing Russian air. Feeling its damp cold. I think about the ubiquitous *matryoshka*—nested Russian souvenir dolls—depicting a society hidden in layers. Intourist will show me the outer layer, the polished one reflecting the ordered, confident Communism I first heard about as a child.

A perky young woman, barely five feet tall, with brown flailing wild curls, two children close to her side, steps in front of me. She's wearing a faux-leather jacket, white blouse, and blue skirt, holding white carnations, peering into my eyes with an alluring wide smile:

"*Izvenitze, pajaulista, vui znaite yesli vashem samalyot Anglichinan?*"

I'm meeting my first Russian, in barely twenty minutes. And an attractive one at that. She's picked me. I want to answer her. From my ten days of Russian study the previous summer, I think she wants to know if an Englishman was aboard our plane. I blurt out in my gar-bled Russian, "*Nyet*, I'm American, *Ya Amerikanski. Nyet Angleeski.*"

"*Spacibo.*" She gently embraces the two children. "Yuri *y* Veroníca, *mon deyti*," she says quietly.

Ah, she's saying "thank you." And these are her children; she's telling me their names.

"*Minya zavoot* Frank," I say as I crouch down to shake their hands, "*Kak vas zavoot?*" I ask their names.

I step away. I stare back at her and her children. I move toward my group, drop my bags and rummage for two pen-pal letters from my students. I rush back to her. I resort to gestures and pantomime, waving my arms, pointing to the letters and to the kids. She takes both letters and slips a scrap of paper into my hands. We part. Yuri and Veronica have two letters from America; I, a crinkled scrap of brown paper with her name, Natasha—and a telephone number. I stare at her as she walks away. Out of the corner of my eye, I see a security guard watching.

ON THE BUS to our hotel, I pondered my encounter as if it had been a dream. I reached into my pocket for reassurance that I had her phone number.

Before signing up for the trip through Bridges For Peace, an international travel agency in Norwich, Vermont, which was handling 10 percent of US–Soviet exchanges, I hesitated because I would be in a group traveling under the guise of the Soviet Union's Intourist travel agency. I recalled Professor Waite's lecture in college about the *pokazukha* of Potemkin villages in which Grigory Potemkin placed a series of facades of buildings along the Dnieper River to impress Catherine the Great and her Russian allies. Would Intourist replicate the Potemkin-village staging? Would it proclaim that all was well in the Soviet Union? Would the bus keep us in front of the red veil, confining us to the polished outer layer of the *matryoshka*? Would I be able to peel back its inner layers?

Not twenty-four hours on Russian soil, and I'd already broken the mold as a tourist. I stood apart from my eighteen fellow travelers. I was eager to get off the bus and be on my own; I hated being told what I was supposed to do. I'd been gregarious since childhood, wanting to meet people, to find out who they were, and to make friends. When

I was four years old, my mother told me that I'd stood naked at the front door of our family's small inn in the Berkshires and intoned, "Hi, I'm Tommy Thoms. Come in. Come in." Quintessentially me, waiting to be smiled at and patted on the head, an early sign that I wanted to be liked. Growing up, I often thought I was on my own path; I wanted to be noticed, to be seen as unique, as my own person. At the same time, I felt my parents thought that I was not "good enough" and "less than" who I should be, a thought I harbored for more than fifty years.

And I was the older brother, who at summer camp sought recognition, only to be placed in right field and batting ninth while my younger brother played center field and batted first. I yearned to be junior-high class president, but it was again my brother, who held no similar ambitions, who achieved that office. And my mother, who seemed to hold higher standards for her firstborn, often criticized me at the dinner table, once sending me away as I overheard her say, "It's a wonder Tommy has any friends given how he treats them!" I raced up the backstairs behind the dining room in a rage, slammed the door at the top shattering one of its four glass panels. Not having friends was something I dreaded.

As I grew up, I learned to derive satisfaction from being different. I owned the only light-blue, three-speed, Norman English bike among my friends' black Raleighs and Rudges. I was loyal to the Cleveland Indians amid rabid Yankee and Red Sox fans. I threw a baseball right-handed but bowled with my left. And among our friends, my family was the only one to have Studebaker Land Cruisers, first a 1948 dark-blue, then a 1950 bright-green bullet-nose. I found pleasure in all these "differences."

My pride in being different—as slight as those differences were— set a precedent. Once I became a teacher, for twenty-five years I made it a point to be one of a kind. Still, I wanted to be recognized for my accomplishments, for my innovative pedagogies. As I look back on the span of my life, I came to see others' judgments as gifts—including admonitions from parents, teachers, coaches, camp counselors, and neighbors on my street—guides to my becoming a better person, a "good enough" person.

I WAS ON Russian soil with the intention of escaping Intourist's directives—*and* I'd met Natasha before I even boarded its bus. But I needed chutzpah to pick up the phone in my international hotel room to call her. I feared either the phone would not operate or would be tapped; the KGB would discover me and send me home. My stomach churning, I decided to call on Sunday, our second morning in Leningrad. I could not pass up this opportunity. I'd had contact with Natasha moments after landing at the airport—actually, she'd approached me—and I didn't want to let her slip away. She was my first Russian off the tour-bus track, a chance to discover how Russians lived behind the red veil. I might not have another chance. If Nina, our hovering *bábushka* tour guide in the proverbial headscarf, discovered my clandestine intensions, she would surely have kept me close.

I took out the scrap of paper from my pocket and dialed the number. Natasha answered but with considerable static. She seemed to recognize my voice. After some confusion—and language help from a friend—I managed to write what I thought was her address. After lunch, Nina gathered our group in the lobby to leave for a Russian Orthodox monastery; I stayed behind and slipped out to find Natasha.

I took my first metro to the Petrogradskaya District with no clue as to where Bolshoi Prospekt might be. An escalator took me deep into the bowels of the city. The roar of the train confounded my ears, and the ride jerked and jostled me and my fellow passengers. Somehow I located the Bolshoi Prospekt stop. Coming up another endless escalator, I stepped out into a myriad of gray buildings, Cyrillic signs, and colorless Soviets rushing about.

Thinking I'd found her address, I took four flights up a dingy, cracked, concrete stairwell with peeling, pale green paint, the air reeking of piss. I hesitated before what I thought was the door of her flat. I knocked. The door opened. Natasha, in a faded, flower-patterned, orange puff-dress and looking even more attractive, again had a big smile; Yuri and Veronica hovered just behind.

"*Priviet,* Frank, *pajaulista, prohoditye,*" she said, beckoning me to come in.

I was in my first Soviet flat! She led me through its small, dark hallway past an unlit bathroom with a rusted cold-water tap but no bathtub or shower, and past a somewhat disheveled galley kitchen with dishes and pans piled high on a counter next to a tiny white sink, a large combination window at the back with peeled paint on the frame, and towels hanging on the open window. We entered a cozy living room–bedroom with a brown oriental-patterned rug wall hanging, a dark mahogany wardrobe in the far corner, a red sofa bed, a curtained window to the north, and a card table with lunch set for four. The air was somewhat musty, the window closed, but the food looked well prepared.

Yuri and Veronica were dressed for the occasion. They kept staring at me as if I were some movie star. Yuri, a skinny eleven-year-old, nearly as tall as his mother and having similar curly hair but lighter, wore an orange-and-white-patterned collared shirt buttoned at the top and dark, baggy, cotton pants. His sister, Veronica, eight, had wavy light hair down to her shoulders and a twisted front tooth and was wearing a thick, white, knit dress with two bluebirds on the collar and several on the hem. They were on their best behavior. Had I had better Russian, I would like to have been able to ask about their friends, school, and what they liked to do.

Natasha was exuberant. She pranced as if on a dance stage, her slender body, perky breasts, and hair flitting about as she served a delicious pea salad, bread, and borsht—I imagined prepared especially for me. I couldn't take my eyes off her; I think she wanted that, as she kept looking at me. Without a common language, our eyes looked to fill in that gap. Her wildly curled hair surrounded her high-cheekbone face and perpetual soft smile. We managed to make conversation—perhaps with different meanings for each of us. After eating, Yuri dressed up in a cardboard-constructed knight's helmet and shield, something he was proud of. Veronica remained quiet.

About two hours later, her husband, Slava, arrived in his Lenin cap and collared black jacket showing a broad grin. (I had thought she might be married as I'd seen men's clothes on the couch and a couple of hats hanging in the hallway. When I pointed to the clothes, she said "Slava, *mi moosh*," which I thought meant "husband.") He stepped back when he saw me. His grin dampened, his eyes unsettled, and he seemed not to know how to react. I wondered if he had known I was coming. He mumbled some words to Natasha and she responded; she became more reserved. I smiled as I shook his hand. Still, he seemed hesitant and moved to the chair near the table. He soon became more comfortable and interjected comments, which I did not understand. By the time I left his broad grin had returned.

I was where I was not supposed to be. Perhaps Slava thought the same.

After leaving Natasha and Slava's flat, I returned to my hotel. Finding no one from my tour, in the fading afternoon sun I boarded a bus filled with men in crumpled suits and head-scarfed women, some holding babies. Several blocks from my hotel, we crossed the Neva River and passed above a construction site. I looked down at what appeared as miniature, riveted, sheet-metal steam shovels, bulldozers, and trucks. All spray-painted dull orange and faded blue—as if in a sandbox waiting for a child's *vroom, vroom, vroom.* That moment etched in my mind. Sensing a nation emulating the West but well behind.

THE DAY BEFORE, our first full day, I managed to slip away from the scheduled afternoon tour. I put on my cranberry Lands' End coat, slung my black camera bag over my shoulder, and left the hotel to locate Nevsky Prospekt, the Broadway of Leningrad. I'd promised friends at home to try to find two Dartmouth students I'd never met—Heather and Carol—who were studying at Leningrad State University. I was to deliver stuffed, mini teddy bears. I had no clue where the university was located—and could hardly read Cyrillic.

Gawking under the warm afternoon sun amid the bustle of Nevsky Prospekt, I spied two young men eyeing me among the crowd. My stomach tightened. I thought about the dollars in my wallet. Nina had warned us not to exchange money on the street—and only spend our dollars at the Beryozka, stores that were for privileged Soviets and foreigners. Assuming the KGB was everywhere, I didn't want to take any chances. The shorter man, in a dark trimmed beard with a receding hairline, approached first; his handsomer sidekick, taller, blond, wearing large, pink-tinted, clear-plastic-rimmed glasses followed.

"Hey, you from America?" asked the bearded one in good English, "I am Alexei and this is my friend Román. Are you looking for Soviet things? We can get them for you."

"No, thank you," I said as firmly as I dared, my stomach still aquiver. Was I in for some trouble? To deflect them from further requests, especially asking to exchange rubles for dollars, I quickly told them of my mission to find Heather and Carol at the university.

"Hey, Frankie from Hollywood, we know these girls," Alexei said with a broad grin. "We are meeting them tonight for dinner." His response etched in my mind.

Yeah, right, I thought. Of the nearly five million people in this city, these two know these girls? And they are having dinner with them tonight? Should I play along? What do they really want from me? My cameras? My dollars? My Lands' End coat? My breath contracted. No doubt I appeared nervous. Yet they seemed friendly enough—and I liked friendly. What could I lose? I'd never find the university on my own. Risky as it may have been, they seemed okay. I started to breathe easier. At least I'd have guides for the afternoon—and besides, Alexei had a car.

But I desperately needed a toilet. Alexei exhorted Román, "Take Frankie to his first real Soviet toilet!" words that still ring in my ears. Román led me down steps to below the street. We entered a dark, dank space with puddles of urine on the floor. Ye gods, I can't pee here, I thought, the smell's unbearable. But barely able to hold it, I followed the stink to a stained tall urinal. Holding my breath while I peed, I quickly retreated. Román grinned.

We walked to Alexei's car, a black Lada, the Russian VW bug. He drove around the city in and out of back streets. In the company of these two black marketeers, I was into a layer of the *matryoshka* inside Soviet life, one verboten to tourists. The more time we spent together, the less tense I became. Alexei and Román were letting me in on a budding capitalist under-culture behind the red veil, which would later rear its ugly head with Putin's oligarchs.

They expressed their mixed opinions about Gorbachev, sometimes saying he was a good Communist, other times a poor leader. Early that evening, Alexei parked his car in a back alley. I wondered where we were. He led us through an unlit back door that opened into a dark, wood-paneled room with a large table, a white tablecloth set with vodka and cognac bottles in the middle. A bright blue Turkish fabric hung on the far wall.

Toward the back, two girls, who looked like sisters, both short, dark hair with bangs, were sitting quietly; they grinned as we walked in. Could these be the girls? Heather? Carol? We looked at each other. Alexei smiled, "See, Frankie, I told you they would be here." Quizzically, they looked at each other, then at me. I reached into my pocket and took out the teddy bears. It all became clear. They practically hugged me for having brought gifts from their friends at home.

By the time we'd spent a couple of hours at the table, having found the girls felt natural. If Alexei and Román had found me, why would they not find other Americans? I never learned how they met the girls, but I was sure that these black marketeers with their excellent English pursued students at the university seeking their dollars. After a delicious dinner and raucous conversation—perhaps it was a private black-market restaurant—Alexei took me back to my hotel. He talked about meeting again, but we never did. No one in my group seemed miffed that I'd been gone. I was feeling smug about my encounter but kept it to myself.

Despite their disparate backgrounds, both Natasha and her family and Alexei and Román had revealed Russian lives. They were products of Communist upbringing, having once been Young Pioneers. Now they had taken their respective paths: Natasha, the housewife living in a regular flat, the mother of two children with a husband who went to work every day, perhaps as a bus driver or construction worker; I never found out. Alexei and Román had chosen a more devious route, savvy about the influx of foreigners and opportunities with their English to get dollars and live more interesting lives.

Meeting Russian people had barely begun.

SINCE A LENINGRAD school was not on our itinerary, I was determined to find a way into a classroom. I hoped to verify the authenticity of my simulated Soviet school day, which I had implemented with my eighth-graders in the early sixties. On my last day, I convinced Natasha—with considerable gesturing—to take me to Veroníca and Yuri's school. After a ten-minute walk, Natasha, in her faux-leather jacket and flowing blue skirt, led me up the concrete steps through a wooden door into a large lobby of a nondescript three-story building. On the stairs, blue-uniformed boys and brown-uniformed girls wearing red Pioneer scarves and Lenin badges were shouting to one another as they rushed past us. Natasha led me through the unexpected melee up to the second floor.

She disappeared down the hall, gesturing for me to stay at the top of the stairs. The din from the children encapsulated me, so unexpected was it. I had imagined Soviet schools as orderly places governed by formal behaviors and rigid rules—as I'd role-played with my eighth-graders. I stood there. An interloper. An embarrassed American looking to connect with them as they rushed past, casting glances at me. I was thinking, Would I see Yuri in his German lesson? Or Veroníca in her primary class?

Natasha reappeared, gripped my hand, rushed me down the stairs and out the door. I'd not taken one picture, spoken to a child, or seen a classroom. It all happened so fast. Had Natasha misjudged? Had we done something wrong? Why couldn't she invite a friend into her children's school? I didn't want to cause trouble. I only wanted to see classrooms. I wondered if I should even have asked her to take me to her kids' school. Yet I felt cheated. If only I could have talked to someone, I would have found a way in. But my verbal gifts were limited. I'd connected with Natasha and her family using my rudimentary Russian, gestures, and pantomime. Now I wanted to use my voice, but it could only speak to me.

She hastened down streets, around corners, past dull carbon-copy buildings, in and out of courtyards, through a maze of broken stuff and refuse of Leningrad's back alleys. I barely kept up with her. Twenty minutes later, she stopped in front of a large brown wooden door, above it a blue sign behind glass: N° 86. She opened the door, and we entered a large, empty, silent corridor.

"*Shkola?*" I whispered.

"*Da, shkola. Moya padrooga robotit stiyeas.*"

"Yes, in a school. My friend works here," I think she was saying.

She repeated her words slowly and added *na bibliatéke*. Ah, we *are* in a school where her friend works in "the library." I relaxed; in silence we walked up to the second floor, down a long dark corridor to a locked door. As we turned to leave, a slender woman in khaki pants with a long cardigan, a scarf wrapped around her shoulders, and carrying a pile of books came toward us and opened the door.

Natasha introduced Anna and briefly spoke with her. We stood in her library, in which I counted fewer than five hundred books and which had no visible audio-visual equipment, no study tables, no workstations—and no children. An empty library. Did this mean that the library was not part of the curriculum? That students were not expected to pursue learning on their own? Soviet schools, as I understood them, were a tool of the State, where learning happened in classrooms from texts published by central authorities in Moscow. Hence, there was probably no time to do research.

Anna turned to leave, locked the door, and led us farther down the hallway to a room with a cracked-open door—a primary classroom. I spied the teacher, barely taller than her children, wearing a dark brown shirtdress. Opening the door, she welcomed us and beckoned us to come in. I recall these moments in her classroom as if they were yesterday.

I stepped to the front of the room. I counted forty-four children in Ocktobrist uniforms, girls in brown dresses and white aprons with white collars and white chiffon bows in their hair, boys in their blue jackets and pants. They all gazed up at me. I was in heaven, my kind of heaven. This is what I came for, I thought.

I took out my camera and took a picture of a row of children standing next to the windowsill: *click*. Another picture of a group standing nearby: *click*. At the teacher's orders, they sat down in unison, two to a desk—just as I'd set up in my simulated classroom— eyes up at me, vinyl bags hanging at the side of the desks, some partially opened, some closed: *click*.

I looked into their eyes. I was the surprise American in his cranberry coat and black camera bag taking pictures of Russian children, a wall-to-wall human carpet. Why they were crowded so close together in this, the largest country in the world? They were standing and sitting down as one, as if tied together. They stared at me. They smiled: *click, click.*

We were about to leave. I bent down to a little girl in her white chiffon ribbon nearly the size of her head.

"*Kak vas zavoot?*" asking for her name in my halting Russian.

She stood, burst into an embarrassed smile, and dropped her eyes. "Katya" . . . or was it "Natasha," "Anya," "Tanya," "Nadia"? I can't remember. Others jumped up, moved closer, relieved from rigid sitting. I heard, "Alyosha," "Polína," "André," "Grisha" . . . all reaching out, no doubt, to their first American. The classroom faded away; it was these Russian children and me. I didn't want to leave.

A girl approached from the middle of the room—perhaps with the teacher's encouragement. In a quiet voice she said, "My name is Mary." In English, perfect English! Our eyes met. A wall vanished. More children shouted their names. It was hard to say *goodbye*, for them and for me. Their eyes asked for more time together. Wanting to get to know the American perhaps. My eyes welled up. I wanted to stay, to learn all their names, to find out what they cared for, what they hoped for. Alas, we had to leave: *click.*

I told this story over and over after I returned home.

Back on the street, I gave Natasha a hug—our first one—and thanked her for giving me this gift. Her courage at the airport had led me to her flat, what certainly must have been a risk, something I did not think about at the time. And she'd contrived a way for me to see a school, meet a librarian, and spend time in a classroom. Another risk. She was fulfilling my desire to meet real Russians, away from my tour bus. She was taking me behind the red veil.

THE NEXT DAY, our group departed by train to Kiev (Kyiv). After touring Saint Sophia's Cathedral, we had dinner in our hotel. Afterward,

I stepped outside to get a feel for the city. A young woman, black-haired, dark-eyed, in a long black coat, approached me. She said in English, "Hello, my name is Lara." She started walking into a nearby alley, and I followed cautiously. She stopped, turned to me, and began telling her story. She had finished school and did not have a job. Before I had a chance to ask her about it, she blurted out, "And I'm a heroin addict."

I froze. What did she want? Was she looking for money? Then I said, "I can't imagine, Lara, what that's like." I didn't know what else to say. Here was this young, attractive Soviet in this Communist country, whose pageantry lured foreigners to admire its successes, telling me she was an addict. I listened to her woes, details that made little sense. Eventually, figuring that I could offer her little solace, she turned and disappeared down the alley.

It never occurred to me that drugs would have been an epidemic in the Soviet Union. State control would surely have prevented it. Lara opened me to thinking more broadly about this intriguing Communist country; how it, too, could manifest its sores like all other countries. For the next two days, I stayed with the tour. I had much to think about from our time in Leningrad and my brief encounter with Lara.

Our group spent its last days in Moscow, touring Red Square, the Kremlin, Lenin's Mausoleum, GUM, and St Basil's. And much to my delight, our guide took us—and the Minister of Education from Sri Lanka—to School N° 40, which turned out to be a show-school, one designed to impress foreigners. We were treated as honored guests and offered glimpses of classrooms. While my tour group had tea with the director, I lingered to watch a lesson with the articulate Tatyana Popelyanskaya and her tenth-form English-language students. A real surprise, because my reading about Soviet education had led me to expect to see her standing up front, dictating the pace, asking questions, students standing to respond, and she accepting or rejecting answers. Instead, Tatyana's lesson was deep in conversation.

It was in Moscow's Red Square where I first felt close to the Soviets. Its regal magnificence, the largest open space of any city I'd seen, drew me in at first sight. The massive Soviet red flag high atop the Kremlin reminded me of the red on the *My Weekly Reader* wall chart in my fourth-grade classroom. I stood in awe on the Square's cobblestone floor, feeling the soul of the country that had become my obsession. At midnight, I slipped away from my hotel and returned to have one last look. The Kremlin's red flag fluttered despite a windless night. I learned later that it had wind holes that pushed out air, a symbol of the red veil *pokazukha*, a Soviet disguised mastery of what it wanted the world to see. Alone, I watched lines of tanks and jeeps roll onto the cobblestones in anticipation of the parade honoring the Great October Socialist Revolution of 1917 the next day. I spied a bullet shell on the ground and put it in my pocket. I wondered if I might have been witnessing something I should not have. But nobody approached to make me leave.

On our last afternoon, we toured the city's massive Pioneer Palace, the showcase of chosen Young Pioneers. In blue and brown uniforms, white shirts, and red scarves, hundreds of children performed behind glass-enclosed rooms for thousands of visitors from around the world—their Lenin badges and red scarves, ubiquitous on Young Pioneer school children, the red bearing the legacy of Lenin.

Taking a break from rushing through the palace, I stopped on a landing and peered through a picture window into a dimly lit large room. A young Pioneer girl, blonde with braids, about ten, alone in the near corner in her brown school uniform, red scarf, white apron, her Lenin badge on the apron's halter, stood before a dozen dolls at miniature desks. As other tourists raced up and down the stairs, I watched.

Standing before her "children," she revealed a curious intensity directing them with attentive, quizzical, scowling looks. She hadn't noticed me. She seemed to be internalizing a Soviet teacher's demeanor. A deep sense of purpose. Devotion. Parental posture. In charge. A Soviet teacher served as a surrogate parent for the State and assumed full responsibility for the patriotic character of her students. Would this child become a teacher?

It was not the way this Moscow child played school that mattered. It was her desire to play school—a hint of a calling—that revealed more than the act itself. This Young Pioneer, a product of a conformist culture, was cloning the actions of her teachers and emulating them well. Yet, she was alone in this room in a glorious palace where groups of other Pioneers were giving demonstrations in bright rooms behind picture-glass windows for visitors to admire. Maybe, just maybe, by being alone she was secretly nurturing her own seed, choosing what she wanted for her own satisfaction—and without pretense.

On our last evening in Moscow, I met Arthur, Andy, and Slava, eager to talk with an American. They lured me by metro to Arthur's sanctuary-room at the edge of the city limits. They inquired about my Western clothes, admiring my jeans and cranberry coat. At first, I felt on exhibit, but that soon faded away. We drank hard-currency vodka, which I'd purchased at the Beryozka shop. I stayed with these budding dissidents until three in the morning; we listened to Elvis Costello, Simon and Garfunkel—and to their criticisms of Gorbachev. Nina, our guide, would have considered my venture off limits, a fragment of Soviet life behind the red veil.

As WE WERE flying home, I thought about my path to this trip. In the summer of my freshman year at Williams College, I had been hired to supervise and care for twenty-five children from six to sixteen from the twenty-fifth reunion class. By the end of the weekend, I was a pied piper, a school of fish swirling behind me. I'd found my calling: I would become a teacher. I'd finish college, then on to graduate school for a master's, and then to the classroom. But in the summer after my first year in graduate school, life took a detour. My wife-to-be and I created our son while making love for the first time in my parents' bedroom. We married the following January in a private Catholic service in her hometown and held a reception at my home. Both of us felt a deep guilt for our transgression.

I continued on to graduate school and earned a Master of Arts in Teaching and a Diploma of Further Study in June 1962. With wife, baby, and a new Volkswagen Beetle, we moved to New Hampshire, where I signed my first teaching contract at Hanover's Junior–Senior High School. Being well integrated into America's patriarchal culture, I was allowed to continue on my chosen path. I was the man of the family, expected to have a job and provide income and security; as a woman, my wife was expected to leave college to be the devoted mother of our son. As shocking and unsettling as our surprise pregnancy had been, it had been a blip on my path, a momentary awakening, and a sudden entrance into adulthood. For my wife, it had changed her life. As I look back on that time, I'm not surprised that after fifteen years we went our separate ways; our kids—a son and a daughter by then—were in middle and high school.

I joined a cadre of liberal arts graduates as a teacher at Hanover Junior–Senior High. The principal assigned me to teach ninth-grade European history and twelfth-grade Problems of Democracy and to select textbooks for each course. Before school opened, I met Del Goodwin, my department chair and soon-to-be mentor. In the course of our conversation he asked if he could co-teach my low-tracked senior Problems of Democracy. Co-teaching with Del, an unimagined concept at the time, changed my teaching life.

In the spring of my first year at a department meeting, Del said, "I want you, Tommy, (he called me by my childhood nickname) to move down to the eighth grade to teach area studies with a focus on Marxism, Communism, Russian history, and the Soviet Union. Your course should be honest. You need to teach your students to understand Marxist Socialism and Communism as sound ideologies, not as evil or bad. Students deserve to know these doctrines for what they are. And to know the Soviet people for who they are. Millions of people around the world subscribe to these ideologies. I believe you are the teacher in our department who can do this."

His request sealed the deal for me. It rekindled my passion for all things Russian. On the first day of the unit in the spring of 1964, I darkened my classroom, pulling down the shades, papered over the glass panel on my door leading to the hallway, and turned off half the lights—the room becoming an inner sanctum. My unsuspecting students stepped in hesitantly wondering, "Why is the room dark?" They might well have asked, "Is Mr. Thoms about to do something bad?"

I switched on the overhead and projected Del Goodwin's "Preconditions of Socialism" on the screen. I wanted to set a tone and have students take these principles seriously. Throughout our discussions, I had no intention of appearing fair and balanced, no intention of entertaining different viewpoints, and every intention of stimulating critical thinking. For the next three weeks, four periods a day, my eighth graders and I assessed Marx's economic determinism and dialectical materialism, his concept of history as progress, the capitalist class structure, the five laws of capitalism, the role of the petite bourgeoisie in oppressing the proletariat, and we concluded by reading and discussing *The Communist Manifesto*. Each time I deepened my own understanding, becoming a knowledgeable Marxist. I was learning as much as my students.

At the same time, I was assessing their reactions. I was impressed with their commitment to engage with the material. We formed a trust, so much so that no parents voiced concerns about my approach. Perhaps some did, but I never heard about them; maybe Del Goodwin was protecting me. Only once did a student break into tears after I had said Marx's tenet that religion is the opiate of the people.

"No, Mr. Thoms," she said frantically. "That's not true! I love my church! My church is not like that! I love it very much!"

I'd hit my first speed bump. As bad as I felt for her, much like a father overstepping his parenting, I sensed that inculcating Marxism was having its desired effect. I took time to console her, gently backing off from the quotation. I said later, "Mary, let's see what Marx wrote about this in *The Communist Manifesto*."

Our work with Marx led into the heart of the unit: a close scrutiny of the Soviet Union. We began with a brief look at Russian history and then delved into Soviet life and culture. In the next month, we invoked a Soviet classroom: students wore Pioneer uniforms, carried out calisthenics in front of the school, and a few acted as teachers. We assessed documents procured from the Soviet Embassy in DC, analyzed the twenty duties of Soviet school children, discussed an anti-capitalist account of growing up poor in America, put on a meet-the-Communists panel for a neighboring junior high, took exams to become Young Pioneers, and published *Iskra—The Spark—* "All the News That's Red We Print," our Leninist newspaper.

It was total immersion. A new way of teaching for me. A step closer to coming to know Russians. The two editorial pieces in *Iskra* indicated how deeply my students and I submerged ourselves in the Marxist-Soviet-Communist mindset.

THE TIME HAS COME

Too long have we waited for this glorifying moment, when the minds of the people shall awaken to the stirring thought of rebellion against the grande bourgeoisie .... Now is the time for you, the oppressed victims of the American grande bourgeoisie, to arise and crush the capitalists with the omnipotent implements of Communism: atheism and materialism

. . . . Citizens of America, ignite, and fight for your rights as a Communist!

WHY?

Iskra is here because the American student has the right to project himself into the pulse of another nation. Iskra is the expression of this right. We have "been" Lenin, Stalin, Marx, and Khrushchev; we have "interviewed" these notables. We have "lived" in a Soviet classroom; we have "felt" the pressures of being dogmatically disciplined.

    Iskra is a privilege. We cherish it.

IN THE 1970s, I returned to teach the gospel according to Marx. I was working in a nontraditional open classroom for fifty-two sixth-, seventh-, and eighth-graders, which had been set up in two adjoining rooms, each with work stations and which included a large meeting area.

I had chosen a new approach. I told students that we would be studying a unit on Marxist Socialism and later Soviet Communism. To set the tone, I designed a questionnaire that had ostensibly originated from the "American Youth Public Opinion Center."

It had fifteen questions, each asking for a "yes" or "no" response. Answering "yes" for twelve of them meant supporting socialist beliefs; for the other three a "yes" meant support of capitalist beliefs. Students were to put a "?" for undecided—which they would later learn meant they were "leaning toward socialism." To make it appear official, I printed the questionnaire on mimeographed paper instead of the traditional purple ditto. I designed the questionnaire to support socialist thinking:

Survey Questionnaire, Middle School Level from the auspices of the American Youth Public Opinion Center (AYPOC), Concord, New Hampshire.

This survey questionnaire is being distributed to selected classrooms throughout New England. It is designed to find out how American youth think about today's world. This particular version has been shortened from one hundred questions to fifteen. We hope you will respond thoughtfully and answer what you think; there are no right answers. Thank you for your time; we will let you know the results.

[Examples of questions]:

1. *Do you believe that every American should get an equitable share (fair share) of goods produced in this country?*

2. *Do you believe that major decisions in society should be made by its most intelligent members?*

3. *Do you believe that the economy should be run by people who are interested in serving the good of the society?*

4. *Do you believe that the main purpose of the police in American society is to protect citizen's property and possessions?*

5. *Do you believe that most of the wealthiest families send their children to public schools and State colleges?*

I wanted to lay the groundwork to encourage conversation about the appeal of socialism as advocated by Marx, a point-of-view obviously contrary to American public opinion at the time. We were still enmeshed in the Cold War with the Soviets. I intended to open students to thinking critically of their assumptions about principles labeled as socialist, which were implied in the questionnaire. After all, millions of people in the Soviet Union, Communist China, and other countries were committed to it.

A week after students filled out the questionnaire, a letter addressed to our principal arrived, signed by the "president" of the AYPOC, J. R. McCarthy. In the letter—which I had written and which I read aloud to all fifty-two students at an assembly—Mr. McCarthy scolded our school principal:

> *Apparently, these children already have strayed from basic capitalistic values and are leaning toward socialist values. Only occasionally have we had students respond to the questionnaire with more than five (5) socialist-leaning responses; yours, however, were all well above that. Thus you can see our concern.*
>
> *We are indeed sorry that these results came forth from your school. Let me say on behalf of my colleagues and the Board of Directors that we shall do anything we can to abate the spread of this disease of the mind that is infecting your children.*
>
> *Yours very truly,*
> *J.R. McCarthy*
> *President*

After reading aloud the letter, I posted it on an easel behind me. Alongside it, I put a sheet listing the name of each student with an "S," or "U" (in red) or a "C" (in black) next to answers to each question. A simple glimpse at the sheet showed an overwhelming number of red "S's" and "U's" indicating answers agreeing with or leaning toward socialist thinking.

I took a deep breath as the room went into a long silence.

Then, Josh, one of my less reticent students, not unexpectedly spoke up. "What do you mean, Mr. Thoms? I'm not a socialist."

"Neither am I," said Lisa, who always held firmly to her beliefs. Students began to murmur among themselves.

"How is that possible? I've never heard much about socialism or Marxism. I never read anything about them," said, Katrina, often skeptical. "This is crazy!"

Stephanie, nearly in tears, said, "That's not possible, I love our country."

Despite these and other angry reactions (which I had not anticipated), I hoped my students would have understood the appeal of socialist thinking through their responses to the questions. Unlike my role-playing with Marxism in the sixties, where we examined socialism as a movement and read *The Communist Manifesto*, by choosing to engage them with this questionnaire, I had stigmatized them as potential socialists. I was deliberately deceiving them. I began to feel guilty, a place I had often put myself in. I wanted to be "the good teacher" always; I would cringe whenever I strayed from that stance. Sitting before my dismayed students, I wished I could have undone my deception. I found out later that my colleague didn't like it either.

On a happier note, I restructured Parker Brothers' capitalist Monopoly into socialist Co-opoly, a less threatening way to explore socialist thinking. The rules specified that players should aim to obtain an equal share of money and real estate. It provoked them to shift their mindset. To play to share rather than to win challenged them and encouraged conversations about the merits of a socialist society vs. a capitalist one. Occasionally, I would sit nearby.

Danny, scowling and clinging to the dice while waving his right hand, said, "I own Broadway and Park Place. I don't want to give up either of them, Sarah, just so you can have more. That's just not fair!"

"But it is fair," replied Sarah, one of my most compassionate students. "If you have wealth, you should share with those who have less. Otherwise the poor will suffer while the rich have it easy."

"Sarah, you're being so idealistic," said Will, always willing to speak his mind. "No way can societies make it possible for everyone to have the same."

"Will is right," added Biff, Will's best friend. "No society can make everyone equal. But we could work toward a fairer society in which everyone has equal opportunity. It would mean that schools would have equal funding, unlike today, as Mr. Thoms told us, where our district has more money to spend on schools than other districts in our area."

Andrea, who often dug deeply, said, "On the board, the one place where rich and poor have equality is in jail. I like the idea of sharing that makes equality possible—at least a possibility for equity."

These kids were really thinking! I felt privileged to listen in—better than to chime in, as tempting as it was.

TEN YEARS LATER, in the mid-eighties, I returned to my Russian/Soviet passion. I chose to explore the US–Soviet nuclear threat, again with eighth-graders. We read and discussed at length John Hersey's *Hiroshima*; I displayed large, graphic, black-and-white images of the bomb's destruction (which disturbed some teachers and parents); and I showed the films *Atomic Café* and ABC's *The Day After*.

What might have been the most harrowing exercise involved BBs. I asked students, who were sitting in a semicircle on the floor, to close their eyes.

After a long pause to bring everyone into the quiet, I dropped a single BB into the bowl . . . . In a deliberate voice, I said:

"This represents Little Boy, the atomic bomb that destroyed Hiroshima, an area as large as our county."

After a long pause . . . I clinked another single BB into the bowl.

"That's Fat Man, the bomb that detonated Nagasaki, again an area as large as our county."

Another long pause . . . I dropped ten more BBs, one at a time, very, very slowly.

"These represent the number of hydrogen bombs that could destroy life on earth."

After another silence . . . I slowly poured the rest of the one thousand BBs into the metal bowl, taking almost half a minute.

"These represent all the bombs that are stored in US, European, and Soviet arsenals."

I couldn't remember a restless group of eighth-graders ever having sat so quietly for so long. Had I scared them? Would they have nightmares? Had I taken the nuclear threat too far? Were some parents correct to think this issue was not suitable for thirteen-year-olds? I began to question my decision to thrust my students into the thicket of arguments about the nuclear threat.

It was time to turn to Marxism and the emergence of the Soviet Union. In part because of the time frame and because I wanted to take a different tack, I invited my students to read and discuss, chapter by chapter, George Orwell's *Animal Farm*. His masterpiece proved more than adequate for probing the Soviet mindset. Once we finished the book, I asked my students to assess its implications in a variety of ways. They could choose to rewrite a part of the book, compose a prologue, add a postscript, or create illustrations, songs, or poems. Unlike a test, this approach allowed me to look in on their thinking about Orwell's remarkable fable.

In March 1985, Mikhail Gorbachev became General Secretary of the Communist Party of the Soviet Union. He appeared to want good will with the West and encouraged exchanges between our countries. Soviet delegates came to my classroom. I saw that now it was my time to travel behind the Iron Curtain, to seek Russians behind the red veil. I would be that gregarious person who sought to know everyone he met, to become their friend. Now it would be with Russians.

WHEN I RETURNED home from my first trip in early November, I invoked the *matryoshka* metaphor to describe Soviet society. Back in my classroom, I shared my newfound insights with my students and colleagues. Using slides, I told them everything: being inside

Leningrad's international airport the first night; meeting Natasha, visiting her flat and then a school; Alexei and Román leading me to my first Soviet bathroom and dinner with Heather and Carol; and Leningrad's regal architecture, Moscow's Red Square and Pioneer Palace. I could barely contain my enthusiasm. I arranged to give a slide-lecture to more than three hundred people at a Dartmouth auditorium. I met with groups at regional libraries and was interviewed in the local paper and on the radio.

In all these venues, people asked me questions: What is it really like behind the Iron Curtain? Are Russians different from us? What kind of society do they live in? What did it feel like to be there? Were you ever afraid? I answered these and other questions as best I could. By the end of December, I'd had my fifteen minutes of fame. I felt like an international Leo Buscaglia, an ambassador of love between our two countries. I was on a mission. I had to return.

With considerable effort, I secured a half-year sabbatical from my school district to clear the way to find my way back. In anticipation, I enrolled in a beginning Russian course at Norwich University's summer Russian School. At the recommendation of a contact I pursued in Washington at the United States Information Agency (USIA), I applied to American Field Service International (AFS), the agency in charge of US–Soviet teacher exchanges, which was funded by USIA. Were I to be placed in a Soviet school, I would have daily access to Russians, to their culture, beliefs, values, hopes, and fears—much more so than as a tourist.

While at the Russian School, I received an unexpected letter from AFS inviting me to be one of six teachers for the following fall. My application had come in over the transom in time to replace a teacher who'd become ill. Serendipity? Destiny? My giddiness barely touched my excitement. I told everyone I saw that day of my news. I called my parents, my kids, and my close friends. In three months I would be teaching in a Soviet school!

II
A MINI-MYTHIC SUPERHERO WRIT LARGE

*"I was a billiard ball cued by curiosity, moving with random aban-
don . . . finding my way into the class collectives, into the private
lives of a few teachers and brave students."*

Diary, November '86

I awoke on the top berth of my compartment on the Red Arrow over-
night express from Moscow. My heart was pounding. I was returning to my favorite Soviet city. This time, I would not be relegated to
a bus or hotel, having to find ways to slip out unnoticed. I would be
in a school, in classrooms with children and their teachers, inside its
bustling life, immersing into its culture. I would meet people I did
not know, yet could not wait to see. Would they like me? Would my
new teacher colleagues accept me? Would students understand my
American English, particularly if I talked as fast as I often did?

I looked beneath my berth to see my escort, Viktor Vladimirovich,
a mustached young teacher of English, who had met me just before
we boarded the train in Moscow. He sat dressed in a blue, oversized,
polyester, pinstriped suit and black tie. He seemed eager to secure our
new friendship. As the train slipped into Moskovsky Station, Viktor

pointed to the platform where city education officials and school department personnel were waiting. Once we stepped off the train, a short, perky, self-assured woman stepped forward in her navy-blue suit, her skirt below her calves, and cocking her head, introduced herself in a high-pitched voice to us three exchange teachers.

"Welcome to Leningrad. I'm Ludmilla Mikhailovna, the Education Board's teacher-exchange supervisor. You are to contact me if you have problems." Continuing in her strident tone, she said, "You are fortunate, too, not to teach each week until Tuesday, because English is not taught in the city on Mondays. And we have arranged for you to observe classrooms during your first week. This will enable you to become familiar with our ways. You will arrive each day at ten o'clock, teach three lessons, and attend one in Russian. Then, you are on your own. Welcome again."

So Soviet. So formal. Short and to the point. Bittersweet.

Viktor introduced me to Irina Nikolaevna, head of the English Department at School N° 185. He whispered to me that Irina had just told him that I would indeed be in his school. I was eager to visit, but Ludmilla had arranged a special tour of the city and declared unequivocally that our delegation needed the remainder of the weekend to rest, then a week to observe and arrange our schedule.

Have a rest? Observe the first week? No way! I thought. I've overcome many hurdles to come here to teach. I'm not going to waste a week, not if I don't have to! And teach only three lessons a day? Not if I can help it. I looked for an opportunity to speak with Irina Nikolaevna. She had already shown a schoolgirl curiosity. Observing her in her dark blue-and-white-flecked wool suit, I immediately felt comfortable with her quiet demeanor, gentle face, and warm eyes peering through large, pink-tinted, clear-plastic-framed glasses beneath her Soviet-dyed, red-orange hair. She spoke in a rounded calm voice, a lilting Slavic–British accent reflecting her deliberate, formal manner.

After a genteel breakfast meeting at the Hotel Baltiskaya, my new home, I whispered to Irina to ask if I might come to her school on Monday morning. I was eager to meet the director and learn how to get there from my hotel. She raised her eyebrows, surprised, I think, at my forward behavior, and lowered her voice.

"That would be fine. Viktor, would you be willing to escort Frank?" (He already knew I wanted to come Monday.)

Monday morning, a memory etched in my mind, as if it were yesterday:

Viktor and I rode up the long escalator of the Chernyshevskaya Metro Station and stepped onto Ulitsa (street) Chernyshevskaya. In between his relentless questions about my life in America, I wanted to know what to expect when we arrived at school. He kept repeating, "Our director, Elvira Nikolaevna, will take care of everything. She will take care of everything."

After four interminable blocks, we turned onto a wide, empty, silent street without a car in sight. Viktor pointed to a large square clock above the entrance to the school, partway down on the left at Nº 33 Ulitsa Voinova (now Ulitsa Shpalernaya), not far—I learned later—from the Bolshoi Dom ("Big House," KGB Headquarters). I lurched ahead, zipped up the concrete steps, and nervously waited for him to open the large wooden door. He led me through a dark vestibule into a narrow lobby to the director's cabinet (these Russians did not use the English word "office").

Irina Nikolaevna was waiting. She thanked Viktor, dismissed him, and opened the door to the cabinet. Just inside from behind a large gray-metal desk, Elvira Nikolaevna stood to greet me, an imposing figure, calm, poised, confident. Her short, curled, brown hair—fifties style—surrounded her wide, blue eyes and smooth, round face. Her black dress with several thin red stripes fell about her plumpness, covering but not concealing. She reached for my hand, looked up at me, offered a hint of a smile, and in high-pitched Slavic

English welcomed me. Her presence filled the room. School N⁰ 185 was her dominion.

She invited Irina and me to sit on maroon, padded, wooden chairs in front of her desk, which had neat piles of paper set to her left, a gray princess-style telephone to her right, and diagonally cracked Plexiglas in between. Elvira asked Irina to prepare three cups of Brazilian instant coffee. Irina returned with Russian black bread and cakes with swirls of pale-yellow cheese and three coffee cups in fine white china with gold trim, seemingly out of place in Elvira's simple cabinet. For the next hour, Elvira did most of the talking; Irina nodded; I asked questions.

I departed early that afternoon carrying under my arm an abridged Soviet paperback of *The Picture of Dorian Gray* and Elvira's kind permission to teach her unsuspecting ninth-form language students at nine the next morning. I felt a warmth from her, a gentle self beneath her brusque, official manner. I sensed she was allowing me, unintentionally perhaps, to slip behind the red veil. We'd disrupted Ludmilla Mikhailovna's instructions that I observe classrooms for a week. As I headed back toward the Chernyshevskaya metro, I was imagining that, in the next two and a half months, I would become a part of a Soviet school, not just play the role of an American interloper. I would be a teacher, an investigator, residing inside the *matryoshka*, penetrating its layers. I would be free to be me.

MY FIRST WEEK was all about the teaching. Elvira assigned me to her spacious classroom on the second floor, the best in the school, lavished with new desks, plants, and posters. Irina, as head of the English department, arranged a full schedule of five classes a day—clearly contrary to Ludmilla's orders—each with up to fifteen students from the fourth to ninth forms. Each class was different, as Irina wanted her teachers to have their students experience "the American." They came prepared with their English-language textbooks on topics including holidays; seasons; Soviet school life, such as "At the Lesson" and "In the House of Pioneers"; and US tales, such as *Uncle Tom's Cabin*.

The first period I discussed *The Picture of Dorian Gray* with Elvira's ninth-formers. I met Natasha, Dima, Nina, Misha, Alexei, Olya . . . students whom I recognized in the corridors during breaks. I was surprised by their antipathy to Dorian Gray's search for eternal youth. Olya mused about aging, that every season had its own beauty. Dima said that beauty did not reside outside but in the soul, and if the soul was good, life was good.

I was so fascinated that I failed to take many notes. I was listening to Russian students rather than reading about them. They were inviting me to consider profound meanings. Perhaps they were luring me into deeper layers of their *matryoshkas*, to know them behind their uniforms. Perhaps they were inviting me to discover the Russian soul—and perhaps mine as well. And it was only my first lesson!

When the younger children arrived, they hesitated at the door before scrambling to their desks. At first, they appeared tongue-tied, but my antics quickly erased our stalemate. I didn't stand still. I drew obscure figures on the blackboard. I leaned down toward them, smiled, and laughed with them—and they with me. The room soon became a flurry of hands thrusting into the air eager to be called upon—the same pattern occurred in each group. Irina sat in the back with their teacher; they often smiled and occasionally whispered to each other.

On Wednesday, Irina arranged an impromptu after-school meeting with the International Club; about thirty students and several teachers showed up. I presented slides about my school and town that Viktor inserted, one by one, into a tiny, ancient projector with a dim bulb. The meeting was formal but with warm exchanges. I figured out later that the International Club was a formal way to entertain foreign delegations—ostensibly keeping them in front of the red veil.

The next day, I took a bus trip with Ekáterina Grekova's fifth form to the outskirts of the city to Catherine's Palace, the tsars' summer residence, and to the Pushkin Lyceum, a school for younger members of the royal family, where Russia's most beloved poet, Alexander Pushkin, had studied. On the bus I sat next to Ekáterina's daughter, Sonja, somewhat quiet but curious. We were out of earshot of her mother.

"Do you like to teach?" she asked.

"Yes, I do. I've done it for twenty-five years."

Most of her questions were about me and my school. And about family life. Then Natasha, who was sitting on the other side of Sonja and seemed more mature than her classmates, asked, "Do Americans know anything about our country?"

From there we discussed our two countries, making comparisons. I only offered descriptive information, hoping to build a trust to speak about deeper matters later.

I WAS "THE teacher from America." In corridors, children darted past me with curious glances. In classrooms, they giggled at my joking, drawing stick figures, and pacing about the room. No matter where I went, I sensed students and teachers looking at me. Perhaps asking questions. Perhaps wondering who I really was. At lunch, colleagues inquired about my life in America. Ekáterina Grekova pushed me to explain technicalities of grammar: "Frank, when do you decide to use 'have' in the past tense?" "Why might you use 'had' rather than 'had had'?" I was at a loss—and embarrassed—not to be able to answer her questions. I was no grammarian; I'd been a history major.

Not only was I "the teacher from America," I also felt as if I were "the United States of America." I was among people who knew about my country only from propaganda: The US army is an instrument of aggression; Soviet vs. US plans for the world: "We spread life, you sow death"; capitalist abundance is only for the rich; the US is rotting; your homeless people live in the streets. These were but a few examples. Students learned such propaganda from Moscow-published textbooks, political information classes, propaganda posters, the newspaper *Pravda*, and State television's nightly news *Vremya*. I wanted to give them a different perspective. I would be a dropped pebble in a pond causing ripples of my America to flow among them.

I managed to navigate these hurdles over that first week. Then, on Saturday, which was also a school day, the school celebrated the National Day of Teachers. Ninth- and tenth-form students—the top of the school and dressed in their best—took over administrative and teaching duties for the 750 pupils. These students prepared the assembly hall for lunch, placing bouquets of flowers on each table along with an abundance of tea and cakes in honor of their teachers. Students gave teachers pale-colored balloons, red and white carnations, and handmade cards. Recent graduates returned to honor their teachers.

I received carnations, perhaps more than my share. Children stepped forward and said in English, "Thank you, Mr. Thoms, for being our teacher." So many of them. Congratulating me for being a teacher! Here I was, an America, from the country of the enemy. Yet how quickly they seemed to accept me. I was a teacher, "the American teacher," a teacher they liked. Whatever barriers there might have been seemed to have dissolved. I was becoming an ambassador.

Toward the end of lunch, Elvira invited me to speak. I thanked them for welcoming me to their school and appreciating my lessons. And I said that I looked forward to the rest of my time with them. I left that day knowing that I'd partaken in a Soviet holiday, not as an observer but as a privileged participant.

I'd become a part of the school. I was on the inside, not a foreign observer but an American teacher invited behind its red veil. I gave multiple lessons, spent time among students in the halls, lunched with teachers, and held conversations with Elvira and Irina in their respective cabinets.

I was a billiard ball cued by curiosity moving with random abandon. For the next two and a half months, I plunged into life at School Nº 185, finding my way into the class collectives and into the private lives of a few teachers and brave students. Irina Nikolaevna granted my wish to be involved for the full day; her frequent insistence that I "have a rest" fell on deaf ears. I taught five lessons a day to more than four hundred children each week, monitored the cloakroom, learned countless first names, played games at recess, had lunch conversations with colleagues, and met students and teachers after school—all the time answering endless questions and asking my own.

IRINA NIKOLAEVNA BECAME my anchor. I never had the impression she was watching me. Despite living in a society where, as one of my Soviet friends pointed out, half the people spied on the other half, Irina acted as a friend and confidante. She glided about the corridors, never raising her voice when disciplining a child. Her teaching was well organized, gentle, and respectful of her students. She was a loving presence.

Hardly a day passed when she and I didn't have extended conversations. Her soft voice and gentle demeanor, the gentlest in the school, created a safe space for us to share our thinking. Each time we spoke, she was open about our relationship. Once she told me, "I like the way you are with our children, Frank. You encourage them to want to learn."

I liked that she was willing to say what she thought about her American exchange teacher. The more we talked, the deeper her comments and the more trust we cultivated.

About midway through my time at School Nº 185, I placed a copy of *Animal Farm* on her desk. Inside its front cover, I wrote:

"My dear Irina, With appreciation for all you've done for me. Love, Frank." The next day late in the morning, she approached me with a worried look.

"Frank, I need to see you in my cabinet right after school! I *must* see you!"

I immediately retreated to a familiar but uncomfortable place in my teaching life. What had I done wrong? Had I been enough? Had I offended a teacher at one of my lessons? Are some students upset? Had I come up short yet again? I could not let go thinking about why she was so distressed. Was it all my fault? After my last lesson, I tapped on the door of her cabinet before stepping in. She was waiting at her desk, her eyebrows scrunched, with the copy of *Animal Farm* trembling in her hand. (In my pocket, sensing this to be a moment, I turned on my Olympus mini-cassette recorder.)

"Frank, I don't know where to begin. I read this last night and could hardly sleep. I cannot keep it on my bookshelf." She was nearly in tears.

I didn't know what to say. Orwell's fable did not mention Russia, Stalin, or the Soviet Union.

"As I read it, I recalled the horrible time of our society before and during the war. I don't want to remember it. I can't put this book on my bookshelf, Frank. I appreciate that you wanted to give it to me, but I hope you understand I cannot keep it."

We looked at each other. She, the Russian who had lived through the horror of Stalin's years, and I, the American who could only surmise the tragedy of that time. She returned the gift she could not accept, with no judgment, no hard feelings. It was a lesson that I've never forgotten, and one that many of us will experience in cross-cultural interactions at some point. We develop a new friendship, we believe we've identified just what will bring us closer, and then we bestow what we think is the perfect gift, one our friend will always remember us by. We are so sure that we don't think to anticipate possible negative reactions—factors that exist entirely outside the burgeoning friendship itself.

Irina was living in a society that almost daily honored the fallen heroes of the Great Patriotic War, but she expressed herself from well behind the red veil, well within the Russian *matryoshka*. A layer most Soviets did not want to talk about. We were communicating on a deeper level. I wanted not to have given her the book. Yet it had brought us closer together.

My relationship with Elvira Nikolaevna began on a high note in her cabinet the moment she warmly invited me to teach *The Picture of Dorian Gray* to her ninth-form students in her palatial classroom. I learned later that she expected me to stay in that room for the duration. And probably stick to teaching three lessons per day as Ludmilla Mikhailovna had intimated at the railway station. (A colleague later said that my coming early and staying late allowed me to poke my nose into places that Elvira might not have wanted me to.) Walking throughout the hallways, I wanted to teach in other rooms that were smaller and less well-lit but felt more authentic. And perhaps I would be perceived less as the exchange teacher and more as myself.

Nearly every day Elvira and I had conversations in her cabinet. She gossiped about angry parents, sassy children, her conniving librarian, frequently ill teachers, wily inspectors from the Education Board, and naive American delegations who visited her school. She never hesitated to offer her opinions, better yet her judgments, a queen on her throne dishing out goodies for her American guest. I imagined she was allowing me to see her Russian persona below the Soviet facade of school director. But unlike my relationship with Irina, she was holding me at bay. Perhaps her role precluded forming a deeper connection. Underneath her evident chutzpah, she might have been shy, reticent to reveal herself. Like the teacher whose gregariousness hides a quiet self, buried deep within her. Still, she shared her views of the ins and outs of School N° 185, her attitude toward Soviet education, and her hesitant feelings about Mikhail Gorbachev.

Elvira knew the "in" stuff about everyone and everything in her domain. And I so wanted to know the "in" stuff, so much so that I would become jealous if someone else knew more than I. I believed having had such knowledge provided me security, at least protection from unanticipated incursions. Being in Elvira's cabinet was like being away from the Intourist bus, privy to the "in" stuff about her school and her insights.

Elvira was the designated outer layer of the *matryoshka* in the school hierarchy, the face of her school, an image she cultivated for more than twenty years. She held a firm grip on its reins and disciplined with a sure hand. Her voice cut through the bedlam in corridors, though she rarely had to use it. At faculty meetings, she chastised teachers who failed to live up to her standards. No one was spared. At one meeting, which I was surprised to be allowed to attend, she demonstrated her control in a high-pitched, shrill voice. (Irina translated for me.)

Pavel Yurievich, you are now back from teaching in Hungary for three years, but you've brought the wrong attitude. You've failed to give any fives [A's] to your eighth form. Natasha Ivanova, one of our very best students, has never received a grade below a five. You don't have to prove your toughness. . . .

Nina Alexadrovna, you failed to discipline Nikolai Konstantinov for his failure to attend your form's Saturday cleanup around the school." [How did she know that?]

And a complete shock, "You, Irina Nikolaevna, have allowed for—I did not hear the teacher's name—to have an incomplete register [grade book] at the end of the term. This is intolerable. Intolerable!"

Elvira spoke as the voice of her collective. Nothing private here. She liked having all eyes on her. She was never at a loss for words. She did not reprimand teachers in her cabinet; she did it in front of everyone. And I never saw a student who'd been sent to her; whatever chastisement was needed happened in front of their peers. The collective mindset. Anyone's business is everyone's business. Half the society spying on the other half. Deep in the Russian psyche. Still there, I'm sure. Collective behavior became embedded in Russia from its tsarist days, an integral part of the *matryoshka*.

After the meeting, Irina shared her side of Elvira's retribution with me. In a quivering voice, she said, "Last month, Frank, this teacher who had the incomplete register suffered the death of her beloved Saint Bernard, had to stay home to care for her daughter's ear infection and her eighty-year-old mother's flu, needed to console her son who returned home after a difficult stint in the army, and was herself in bed with the flu!"

Irina expressed her empathic self to me but would not reveal it to Elvira at the meeting. And she said nothing to me about Elvira's rebuke. Perhaps she saw it as Elvira's way to remind the staff that she alone was in charge—how unnecessary, as everyone knew. Irina never said one bad word about her.

A few older students dared to confide about Elvira. Alyosha, a bright, curious ninth-former with budding dark facial hair, told me in a low voice that Elvira spoke with a forked tongue and pretended to support democracy with great enthusiasm in public but held a different personal belief. His classmate Olga, dark haired with deep-brown eyes, and a well-respected student, said that she overheard Elvira mouthing platitudes about the school to foreign delegations, things that had no connection to reality. Any of us who has had an Elvira as a boss at some point might feign admiration but scorn her at the same time. Nevertheless, she reminded me of one who could keep all her balls in the air while maintaining an even presence, like a mother who makes life safe for her children.

Elvira ruled with a carrot and stick, her way to exert control and keep everyone off balance, a well-known practice in Communist circles. Her policies toward school disco parties were a case in point. Twice she canceled a class's party at the last minute for what she perceived as bad behavior—no one was quite sure why. Another time, out of the blue, she rewarded another class by granting permission late in the afternoon for them to hold a party that evening. Demonstrate good behavior in the eyes of the director, and the party's on!

And no one disputed Elvira.

Her unpredictable tactics enabled her to maintain control. For example, she "looked through her fingers" (pretended not to see) when students wore pins on their uniforms other than the proper Lenin badges. But when an inspector from the Education Board noticed this infraction, she reinstated the protocol, which was written in the students' record books: "Students are to arrive in the school uniform without adornments."

It was a *pokazukha,* a pretend action, to demonstrate to the inspector that she was a proper director. Meanwhile, students passed me in the corridor flipping the underside of their lapels to reveal pins I'd given them—ones appealing for peace and friendship, some that Elvira herself had worn. If it served the school—and her—well, she wouldn't hesitate. We wonder, then, when we are with such people, if they are being honest with us.

Acting as a Soviet autocrat, she reflected a society that had lived under totalitarian rule from 350 years of Mongol subjugation followed by centuries of tsarist control. Lenin and Stalin's Soviet Union, proclaiming to build Communism for everyone, perpetuated this embedded pattern.

Elvira ruled in a society corrupt with hypocrisy, burdened with rules and regulations. It showed up in students defying protocol.

Pinning buttons under lapels was only one of many insolences: skipping lessons, copying homework, cheating on tests and exams, and wearing improper uniforms are other examples. Feigning sickness was a favorite for both students and teachers.

Quiet defiances brought life to the boring repetitiveness, the strict protocols, the rigid rules of the system. They made life work. Spending time with students outside of school, I learned more about what it meant to be Russian. The more I asked questions and listened, the more they shared. When they told me about "bad things," I never judged. We developed trust. They spoke about subversion, sharing homework, creative rebuttals to teachers, and imaginative ways to cheat on tests and exams. They never wanted to talk about their lessons. Their defiant behaviors were a microcosm of Soviet society, its people behind the red veil.

Elvira was a legend with parents. Graceful with words, direct with opinions, she shone in charged situations. In the fall, she orchestrated three General Class Control meetings with eighth-form parents. She was laying the groundwork for the next spring's meeting when she would tell one-third of them that their children would not be allowed to continue at the senior level in her school—ostensibly because of overcrowding. Options for these students would be to attend a common school, enter a training institute, or join the workforce. By keeping only selected students, her special English-language school would appear more prestigious.

At one of these meetings with more than fifty parents sitting attentively, Elvira occupied a straight-backed chair on a raised stage, her ankles crossed to one side. Sporting a navy-blue suit with shiny buttons aligned off center and a black-patterned shawl across her shoulders, she spoke in a hushed tone, taking only occasional glances at her notes or the class registers. Her voice was firm and clear. She had a presence that made her appear above those around her, making them look up in deference, ready to acquiesce to whatever she said.

And with those parents, she spoke as if she'd rehearsed each report (Irina translated for me). Looking directly at each student's parents, she said,

Your daughter, Anna Pavlovna, was not ready with her home-work in twenty-five of thirty-four lessons in mathematics, and two times she was without her book, three times without her exercise book.

Dima Vladimirov missed fifteen lessons of English and never produced a note from you, his parents. He has also been disruptive in Pavel Yurievich's geography lessons.

Gregory Mikhailovich, once one of our shining students, has chosen not to do his homework for the past month in English, Russian literature, mathematics, and physics. How can you, his parents, expect him to continue in our school?

It was the same for all of them. No hesitation to castigate. Again, nothing private here. The collective does not allow for individual discretion. Nor for dialogue. Elvira had already made up her mind about students, who would have to leave and who could stay. In the collective, she was the dictator. To be in the collective meant obedience. How amazing, I thought, that this school director, a bureaucrat in a collective state, could assert such personal control. It seemed she could act in any way she chose—like the very wealthy in America, who operate within their own set of rules. I think she believed that she had earned the right to do most anything she wanted.

Her teachers spoke of her in glowing terms.

"I can't understand how she always looks fresh and beautiful, Frank. I'm not always in a good mood, but she always is, especially about her face and appearance."

"Yes, she has a special attitude," said another. "She knows all the children by their family names, by their surnames, what conditions they live in including the grandparents, and the history of each family. She speaks to them in a gentle tone, like their *bábushka*. Many parents come to her and share all their personal problems, about husbands and wives and mothers-in-law. She knows everything!"

"Nothing seems to bother her," said another teacher. "She is amazing. How can she keep it up every day? She is always so fresh and so smart."

Knowing all families enabled her to maintain her authority. Parents were beholden to her. To defy her could result in expulsion of their child. We all know the Elviras in our lives. The grandmother who rules without dissent. The father whose children do just what he says when he speaks. The teacher who never needs to send a child to the office. People's comportment around Elvira reflected the Russian propensity to obey and laud their leaders: for instance, the countless hours in which people wait in line without prompting in Red Square to pay respect to their dead Lenin lying in a crystal crypt in his red-hued mausoleum.

As I look back on our conversations, my life at School N° 185 had two foci. The first, the teaching. The other I did not anticipate, the politics. I immersed myself in my teaching without giving much thought to the impact of my presence. I paid scant attention to how people might have been perceiving me, particularly Elvira and Ludmilla Mikhailovna of the Ministry. Was I inside a bubble of my creation? Would my naiveté come to haunt me?

As the weeks passed, Elvira would talk to me more as an American friend than as her exchange teacher. By revealing her opinions, I think she was looking for mine. The more we discussed, the more I could see her politics, the freewheeling director clearly in charge but hesitant about Gorbachev's reform efforts. She was inviting me—with all the cards in her hand—to probe political opinion in her country. Was she allowing me into private layers of her *matry-oshka*? It felt like that. Time would tell.

In my two and a half months at School № 185, I'd been part of a mutual love affair, immersed into the inner worlds of its teachers and children. At first, I was "the American," even "the United States of America." But by the time my exchange ended, I felt I'd become "a mini-mythic superhero writ large"—an odd term perhaps, but one that seemed appropriate, especially after the farewell concert given for me on my last day. Elvira and Irina arranged a two-hour event in my honor. Children from all grades showered me with poems, plays, dances, gifts, flowers—and tears. As I was leaving for the last time, they asked that I always remember them. Many pleaded for me to return. "Please come back and share lessons with us, Mr. Frank." "Come back to us, Mr. Frank, we'll be waiting for you." I would vow to do just that.

I shared my fondness for School № 185 whenever I could. I gave talks with slides and artifacts to more than two thousand people throughout New England, some audiences over three hundred. I was interviewed again by local radio. *The Christian Science Monitor* wrote a feature article about me. All the while, the children's pleas echoed in the back of my mind. I could only think of one thing: how to return to School № 185 the next spring.

III
A FRAUGHT RETURN

I was challenging the Soviet veneer. Poking my nose where it did not belong, operating as a free spirit, threatening those I cared about . . . .
I was acting ahead of the Soviet change timeline.

Diary, June '87

Returning on my own would be a challenge, perhaps bordering on the absurd. However, in my last weeks, in conversations with Elvira and Irina, I had begun exploring the idea of returning in the spring. Despite their resistance, with each conversation they had hinted that they might support my coming back.

One afternoon—my third or fourth time broaching the subject (turning on my mini-cassette recorder in my pocket)—I brought it up again.

"And when I come, Elvira, I could volunteer every day, all day."

"Oh no, if you come, we will have to pay you."

"That's okay with me. You know how your teachers complain that they don't have enough experience with native speakers. They've told me over and over that they want to know more about the language and the American way of life. I could be that resource. And besides, you know you have a problem with absenteeism. Irina tells me at least once a week, 'I am sorry, Frank, would you be so kind as to take Ksenia's—or Ekáterina's, Elena's, or Anna's—pupils as she is out today?'"

"No, Frank." Elvira's voice was firm and stern. "I cannot invite you!"

And so it went; whatever my argument, Elvira rebutted. Irina listened.

I was asking the impossible but didn't realize it. I viewed problems as opportunities, open to solutions; I believed that I was reflecting Gorbachev's desire to look for possibilities, his apparent desire to let down the red veil. After all, Elvira and Irina valued having me on staff filling holes that would not have been filled had I not been there for the ten weeks. The solution was simple. Invite me to come back, and I would continue to work as I had.

But that was not the Soviet way. Despite Gorbachev's desire to open his country, solving problems outside the system might threaten the Communist Party and prove it wrong. Elvira, who seemed to have shared whatever was on her mind in our frequent talks, acted as if she were boxed in, held back from speaking her mind. She was not free to do what she wished; she had to function within Party rules. She insisted that an American could teach in her school only if Moscow gave sanction. I could come again as an exchange teacher. Otherwise, no, I would be persona non grata. And had she invited me, she might well have been chastised. That was the system.

After Elvira turned me down, I reluctantly telephoned Ludmilla Mikhailovna, the teacher-exchange supervisor at the board. Maybe—a big if—she might have a way to invite me to come. Alas, it was another, "No, Frank, I cannot invite you." ("No" had been her litany with the bothersome me.) Still, I persisted. Ludmilla did consent to have me meet with her supervisor a few days before I left—just in time to run out of time! The meeting lasted twenty minutes. No surprise: "You must go to the Ministry of Education in Moscow, Mr.

Thoms. They must invite you." He provided no name, no telephone number, no address, only "the Ministry of Education in Moscow."

I was stuck in a revolving door. Little did I know how revolving it would become.

BEFORE FLYING HOME, my fellow exchange-teacher colleagues from other cities and I returned to Moscow. I asked our guide to arrange a meeting with a bureaucrat at the Ministry of Education. After finding my way—again struggling to read Cyrillic—I stood in a stark room before a balding short man with horn-rimmed glasses and a baggy, dark-blue suit sitting behind an empty desk.

"We wish we could help you, Mr. Thoms, but you must ask our embassy in Washington for permission to teach in Leningrad. We can do nothing."

I was in a catch-22, an odd person who did not fit into the Red Square structure, a faceless bureaucracy that protected itself. I'd come to a bureaucratic layer in the *matryoshka*, where people seemed afraid to make decisions, a place where nothing could move.

Returning home, I traveled to the Soviet Embassy in Washington. I met with Greg Guroff, director of President Reagan's United States–Soviet Exchange Initiative created after the Geneva Summit.

"Your request is too touchy for the time," Guroff said. "We feel that we cannot press in such a matter as yours. Our negotiations with Gorbachev's people are still fragile." Another "No" from another bureaucracy, this one in Washington.

Meanwhile I made phone calls to AFS asking to be included in the next exchange delegation in the fall. Having seen AFS's International Newsletter piece, "Frank Thoms, Fragments of a Hologram," I thought I might have a chance:

Frank, you see, is a remarkably determined person with a very clear sense of who he is and what he wants . . . He listens with the same intensity as he talks and responds easily to any nuance in a question or comment. Saying "No" to Frank when he is determined to reach a goal is like saying "No" to a force of nature.

[The article concluded with my own words.] "My experience is a piece of the truth of what the Soviet Union is really like. Like a fragment of a hologram. And if I am clear about what I've seen, and very careful how I tell people about it, then maybe we will be able to see the whole picture."

I was grateful for their kind words. But I did not give up on returning to School N° 185 on my own. I secured a tourist visa, and with help from a travel agency in Cambridge, made reservations at the Hotel Leningrad for the last two weeks of May. I would be at the school for its closing weeks and able to attend the "Last Bell" ceremony (graduation). I'd written Irina of my intentions, but her discouraging response arrived two weeks after I'd left. And I'd considered telephoning or telegraphing ahead but decided against it.

I was bucking protocol. But I wanted so much to believe that if I showed up on my own, it would dissolve all barriers. They would know that I'd come for them and welcome me. They would remember my teaching and my desire to commit to the school. School N° 185 had been my channel into learning to know Russians. I was convinced that going back would take me further behind the red veil and deeper into the *matryoshka*.

I woke up that first morning and looked out from my sixteenth-floor window across the Neva River toward the Bolshoi Dom and Ulitsa Voinova. I imagined sitting with Irina in Elvira's cabinet, like that first Monday in the fall when we subverted Ludmilla Mikhailovna's insistence that exchange teachers observe for a week. And Elvira, letting go of her inhibitions, would instruct Irina to make a teaching schedule for me for the next two weeks.

My intuition told me not to call, as Elvira might insist that I telephone Ludmilla to make my visit official. Such consent might take days to secure—if it were even possible. Once I stepped into Elvira's cabinet, I might have a better chance to circumvent the system. I planned to arrive at ten o'clock after Elvira and Irina had given their first lessons.

As I turned the corner at the far end of Ulitsa Voinova, across from the Bolshoi Dom, I spotted Ekáterina Grekova and her now-sixth-formers on the other side of the street. I saw Leena's broad smile. Then spunky Natasha! Little Luda! Chubby Zorab! Tall and lean Natasha! Sergey, his glasses slipping off his nose! Alyosha! Katya! Volodya! And winsome Sonja, Ekáterina's daughter! They'd been my favorite fifth-formers! We'd had a bus trip together and some wonderful lessons.

I took a step off the curb. The children continued to follow Ekáterina. A few waved meekly. No one approached. Ekáterina made no acknowledgement and abruptly disappeared into a courtyard, the children dutifully following her. I looked at where they'd been. Gone. No contact. Nothing. And I was across from a KGB camera attached to the corner of the building.

A few moments later I stopped at the front door beneath the square clock at 33 Voinova and pulled to open it. It was locked! Does Elvira know I'm here? Does the KGB know? I took a deep breath, my hands sweating. I then remembered the door was always locked an hour after school opened. I walked around to the back entrance near Elvira's cabinet, opened the door, slipped through a small dark passageway, and saw Marina, Elvira's secretary, at her desk.

Pointing to Elvira's door and putting my finger to my lips, I asked in a hushed whisper, "Elvira? Irina?"

"*Da*," Marina said smiling.

I knocked gently and called, "Irina?" I waited.

"Frank? Is that you? Frank?" Irina, my ever-supportive

confidante, exclaimed as she opened the door to invite me in. Elvira remained at her gray metal desk, now set in the far corner. A grim look. No greeting. A short silence.

"Are you on tour, Frank?" Elvira asked in her high-pitch voice.

"No, as I promised, I've come to work with your teachers and students for the next two weeks."

"Then, Frank, you better call Ludmilla Mikhailovna. Now!" She turned her gray princess telephone toward me and lifted the receiver. I shouldn't have been there. Involving Ludmilla might let her off the hook for my being in her school without official permission.

Later, after I'd tried to reach Ludmilla, she calmed down. It was as if I'd been there the day before. "You know, Frank, we are in the last week of lessons, practically, and we must prepare for exams. The Education Board for the first time will not tell us the questions until the day of exams. We are all worried. Teaching classes at this time would simply be too disruptive."

Was she diffusing her shock of seeing me? I pondered. Was she indicating that she wasn't surprised? I couldn't tell. Elvira was the master of disguise, a true Communist. She might well have been coming from a layer of the *matryoshka* she'd not revealed.

LESS THAN A half hour later, I stood under the clock at 33 Ulitza Voinova. No *Picture of Dorian Gray* under my arm. No plans to teach. Only Elvira's hesitant consent to allow me to come a couple of times during the week to meet with some students and teachers. And, fortunately, she would allow me to attend the Last Bell ceremony. She told Irina to arrange everything. Not to let me come at all would have been rude. Elvira never wanted to be seen as rude, and by allowing me to come a few times, she may have felt sympathy for my plight.

I'd traveled six thousand miles and spent $3,000 of my savings, which included $135 per day for a small hotel room, far above the ruble exchange rate. As I walked back to my hotel, I recalled the two-hour concert in the fall of songs, poems, stories, and mini-plays in my honor—and the pleas from children and teachers.

At least I would have some access, but Elvira had shut the door on teaching. Were her hands tied even if she wanted to open the door for me? Was her telling me to call Ludmilla Mikhailovna her way to pass the buck? Did she have any choice? I'd never seen her hesitate, almost losing her composure. Perhaps she was allowing me some access to the school under the guise of my being a tourist; foreign tourists frequently came, as it was one of the city's showpieces.

I walked slowly back to the hotel to have lunch. I called some Russian friends to seek solace. One teacher's comment surprised me. "Oh Frank, you are naive to think they liked your way of teaching. Irina Nikolaevna *never* liked what you did." I hung up the phone and slumped onto the bed. Had Irina been acting all that time, treating me as a friend but actually only fulfilling her assigned role? And the concert in my honor, the pleas to come back, was it all *pokazukha*, a show to deceive the American, to pretend that he had special access to the inner workings of the school? I felt tears rising but stopped them almost as quickly. I may have been naïve, but not that naive. Just the warm way Irina greeted me this morning—she couldn't fake that. And she couldn't have faked it every day last fall.

I called my best friend, Misha Baushev, who further consoled me. That evening, Misha, who had a gentle demeanor, wit, and much wisdom, offered to go to dinner and afterward took me to his favorite *banya* (steam bath).

"I'm so glad you've come back, Frank. Natasha [his wife and an admired math teacher at the school] told me that Elvira and Irina were in a state of shock when you appeared. They didn't know what to do."

"Yes, Misha, I gathered that. I thought I could just come back and everything would fall into place. That's not going to happen. But I'm here and I'm really glad. I intend to make the most of it."

As we sat in the sweltering steam, Misha pounded my back with birch boughs until it tingled, and I pounded his, and once saturated with a light stinging pain and heat, we would leap in and out of the frigid bath—again and again. My psyche was restored.

THE NEXT DAY I arrived just before nine for a scheduled meeting with the ninth form, some of whom had been among my favorite students last fall. Irina, who was waiting for me in the vestibule, smiled and reached out to touch my arm.

"I'm so glad you're here, Frank. The students will be waiting for you."

Just like Irina. Friendly, soft-spoken, almost affectionate. My Irina Nikolaevna. She turned to lead me to the assembly hall. A few of the students entered, but they behaved as if held by a force field. No one approached to say hello. It was as if we'd never met. They sat, silent, even Vika, Yulia, Alyosha, and Dima who had been special friends since my first days last fall. Other students, some of whom I had also taught in the fall, began to scramble in. Irina leaned and whispered, "Please excuse the confusion, Frank. We have more students than we expected. Their teachers are absent. Would you be so kind as to speak to all of them?" Here I'd thought I would have an opening to rekindle my relationship with my friends in the ninth form. We'd have a chance for an intimate and honest conversation, a recollection of our good times together. Then all these other kids came in. It was way too large a group to have a conversation. Now I would have to give a speech. Irina stood to address the students:

"Good morning, pupils. You remember Frank Thoms. He has come back to Leningrad as a tourist and has been kind enough to come see us. He is willing to speak about his time in America since he was here in the fall. Please welcome him."

Irina spoke as if we had just met: I, an American tourist, she, the official greeter. But this Irina, my trusted confidante in the fall, was not voicing what was in her heart. I could feel it. Oh, how I wished I could have poured out my admiration for her in front of the students! She had never questioned my motives. We'd developed an intimate trust.

But the bureaucratic system dictated that she had to imply I was a tourist, not a returning friend and teacher. Was I back in Gorbachev's Soviet Union? The one I'd been in last fall? For the next hour, I spoke, but have no memory of what I said. The students acted as if we'd never met. Perhaps Elvira had told them not to engage with me. Perhaps it was because there were so many in the hall. I was beginning to doubt my decision to return.

On my way out, during our conversation, Irina said that five of the twelve English teachers were ill. Had Elvira and she been willing—or, more likely, able—they could have asked me to fill in. But their hands were tied by a reluctant bureaucracy that not even Gorbachev's Soviet Union could loosen. As I was leaving, Irina took me aside and whispered, "You know, Frank, what I like about you is that you know what you want, and you get it. You also sense a situation for what it is. You understand the situation very well." I was not so sure.

THE NEXT MORNING I awoke from a restless sleep feeling the full impact of my isolation. Instead of heading out to teach at School N° 185, I was in a stark room in an international hotel. Rummaging around my suitcase, I picked out the bag of Viking Runes and commentary by Ralph Blum, which a friend gave me before I left; I'd brought them to share with Russian friends who liked the occult. Not familiar with the runes, I decided to reach into the bag and take one. I picked "Ansuz Reversed" and read its accompanying message:

> *You may well be concerned over what appears to be failed communication, lack of clarity, awareness either in your past history or present situation. You may feel inhibited in*

*accepting what is offered. A sense of futility, of wasted motion,
of a fruitless journey may dismay you. Remember, however,
that this is one of the Cycle Runes. What is happening is your
process. If the well is clogged, this is the moment for cleaning
out the old. Reversed, Ansuz is saying: consider the uses of
adversity.*

I read it a second time, and then a third. It began to make sense.
Throughout my life I had preferred not to settle for what was not
working, but to take action. I would have jumped out of bed, dressed,
and bolted out of the room, perhaps made a telephone call, or even
gone to the Education Board to confront Ludmilla Mikhailovna or
the director. Or returned to Elvira's cabinet to plead my case. The
rune gave me pause. I decided to wait, to evoke non-action in the
Taoist lexicon, and *consider the uses of adversity.*

I contemplated my insistence on returning to School № 185 on
my own. Had I been foolish in thinking I could inveigle my way in,
simply because *I* wanted to? How often have I acted without taking
others into consideration? How often have I ignored realities around
me? My decision to follow the rune, to consider the uses of adversity,
provoked me to explore my *matryoshka,* alone on the sixteenth floor
of the Hotel Leningrad.

THE QUESTION OF my return had been a lack of communication from
the beginning. When saying goodbye in the fall, I had no idea that
appeals for me to return were out of the question. I felt bad thinking about the children who were acting as unintentional Pinocchios
pleading for me to come back. I'm sure they thought it possible, as did
their teachers. Why not? I'd been a teacher and a friend, an American
who given his all for them.

And my vow had been real. Had Irina Nikolaevna's letter arrived
before I left, I still would have come: "As for you coming to our country,

Frank, you'd better try to arrange things officially, because unfortunately I cannot send an invitation to you. Besides, it's not my prerogative. Nor is it Elvira's." Although Irina was reflecting what people had said in Leningrad and Moscow—as well as in Washington—her letter would not have deterred me. Maybe the rune was right: "What is happening is your process. If the well is clogged, this is the moment for cleaning out the old." It was time to wait. No more pleas. No phone calls to Ludmilla. No rushing back to Elvira's cabinet. Just wait.

To wait. Really? To wait? Waiting is useless, as if to do nothing. But perhaps the rune is offering me another path, an opportunity to let "what is" take its course, to be nonjudgmental. Ironically, it might be a new way for me to know Russians.

Elvira, Irina, and I had no choice. We were constrained by entrenched bureaucracies, a stagnant layer of the *matryoshka* in the Soviet Union, and by Washington's own bureaucratic structure.

After all, I had chosen to return to Leningrad, to a city cloaked in the USSR, a closed society deep inside a closed society. Nothing came easily, not for Russians and not for me. The Soviet shell polished by space spectaculars and superpower status masked its impoverished second- or even third-world status. But Gorbachev's Soviet Union was beginning to crack open, to look inward, perhaps find freedom, to accept the pain of understanding itself in relationship to the greater world.

I was challenging the Soviet veneer. Poking my nose where it did not belong, operating as a free spirit threatening those I cared about. Behind all the joy and good will showered on me in the fall, my Soviet friends might have felt a need to cling to the red-veil veneer that Gorbachev was asking them to shed. He'd already introduced *perestroika* and was about to implement *glasnost*. I was acting ahead of the Soviet-change timeline. Had I understood the situation, would I have been more restrained?

BEING A RUSSIAN in the Soviet Union was difficult. It was hard to find what one needed, to figure out the rules, to separate fact from rumor, to move from one place to another, and perhaps—as I'd learned the hard way—to get direct answers. And in a foreign country and without language proficiency, we feel this same helplessness. That's why many travelers prefer tour groups, where they feel they have a semblance of control.

I remember in order to send books home, I had to go to three different windows in a post office, unwrapping and rewrapping my package each time. We can barely imagine such a situation because we live in a country where mailing is a simple act. But the Soviet Union was a society in despair, staggering from the imbalance of its past. And surrounded by scarcity. Never enough buses, taxis, toilet paper, clothes, books. No shopping malls, cable television, and no temperate climate.

Not a day passed that most Russians did not think about food. Trips to the produce shop meant there might be cabbage or beets or carrots and certainly potatoes. Or the last bottle of milk or, in the next shop, the last roll of toilet paper. No convenience here, no finding what you want when you need it. No slipping into something comfortable. No peace and quiet. Except perhaps inside your cozy flat, having a quiet conversation in the kitchen. Or in bed. Inside your head. Perhaps not even there. I felt the Soviets' plight. It seemed as if the government wanted them to be distracted and consumed by having to maintain daily life. I often thought about my women teacher friends, who taught all day and still managed to feed their families.

It was in flats that I found—though I did not realize it at the time—much of what I was looking for. Here, in cocoons behind the red veil, people lived away from the public eye of Big Brother, from the ever-lurking Soviet veneer of Lenin statues, propaganda posters, war memorials, tired buses and trolleys, deep escalators built

through the city's marshy soil leading to noisy metros, the hum
of four-door boxy Ladas in the streets, and pedestrians in somber
clothes walking in straight lines—except for the drunks—all going
who knows where.

Inside flats—one, two, or three rooms—were similar furniture
and decor. Dark-veneer wardrobes; deep-red upholstered couches
that folded out into beds; faux-oriental rugs hanging on the wall; and
kitchens with tiny white stoves, linoleum-top table and metal chairs,
a small fridge, and windowsills laden with food. In communal apartments, families shared kitchens and bathrooms.

Yet the Russian people emanated warmth and generosity.
Conversation, vodka, cognac, bread, *pelmeni*, *blini*, pea salad—food
secured and prepared over days—graced tables that in the evening
were garnished with laughter, listening, and respect. Even when only
Russian was spoken, I felt drawn into their private worlds—sometimes I felt I belonged. Feeling we belong in a foreign culture means
we have to give up insisting on being who we are. We need to let
go, dive in, and swim around to let what happens happen. Barriers
drop, and as our hosts' generosity welcomes us while we extend our
appreciation, the commonness of life weaves in and out. We feel submerged if only for moments. Moments we never forget.

THE THIRD MORNING, I waited in my hotel room, skipped lunch, and
shortly before three o'clock left for School N° 185 having received
Elvira's permission for a meeting with the eighth-formers. It was
another group I'd been close to. Upon entering the vestibule, I met
Dima, dark haired, veiled mustache, short, a student from the form
whom I'd known well.

"Hello, Frank!" he said excitedly. "You are back! So glad to see
you, so glad," and then he dashed off. I followed him to the assembly hall where I found Irina. She whisked me inside where the students were waiting, this time only the eighth form. The rest of the

children had gone home. After she greeted me, not skipping a beat, she repeated her introduction:

"You all remember Mr. Thoms. He has come on a tour and has been kind enough to visit our school and talk with you." Judging from the looks in their eyes, they did remember, but they remained quiet and taciturn. In my opening remarks, I was unable to rekindle the energy, the symbiosis of the previous fall. Was I naive to think that we could pick up from where we'd left off? Did I think that my reappearance would be enough to rekindle our friendship? But I, too, hesitated to be myself, feeling repressed, restricted by that Soviet bureaucratic control I knew so well. Our conversation was a blur.

Before I left, I told Irina that I was still willing to come to the school at a moment's notice—and slipped her a scrap of paper with the telephone number of my room.

The next morning my telephone rang.

"Hello, Frank? It's Irina. Why aren't you here? We are expecting you."

After a shocked "Thank you," I hung up, leapt out of bed, dressed, put on my olive-green jacket, gathered my camera, raced out of the hotel without breakfast, ran along the embankment of the Neva, crossed the Liteyny Bridge—trucks and buses belching clouds of black smoke—grinned as I passed the Bolshoi Dom's cameras, dashed up Ulitsa Voinova, darted up the stairs under the clock at Nº 33, and opened the door to find Irina waiting to take me to Nina Alexandrovna's fourth form.

After two lessons with the absent Nina's groups, I reconnected with the diminutive Raisa Vladimirovna, my friend and favorite teacher, and her sixth form. Then onto Ekáterina Grekova's tenth form where I observed preparations for the Last Bell. She was surprised to see me, as she thought Leningrad schools were closed to foreigners from the beginning of May; maybe that's why, when she was with her sixth-formers, she hadn't acknowledged me on Ulitsa

Voinova two days before. Nobody ever seemed to have the same information—perhaps an intentional Soviet means of control, a part of the *matryoshka* that included the KGB.

Irina was behaving like her old self again, pleased to arrange my schedule. Her eyes sparkled. And she kept calling me her cousin, which vindicated our warm relationship—if anyone needed to know that. After a full day of teaching, I left in the afternoon to walk with my friends, ninth-formers Nikolai and Roma. They showed me the memorial to the Young Pioneers of the Great Patriotic War with red carnations placed on a slab beneath the low relief of a Pioneer boy.

That evening Misha Baushev took me to his parents' flat to have supper along with his brother and sister-in-law. I was again a world away from the ubiquitous Soviet red-veil veneer. After an informal meal of meat, bread, pea salad, and ice cream, we adjourned to his granny's bedroom. In her frayed gray robe, her wispy white hair surrounding her wrinkled face, she sat next to a dirty window, her room smelling of urine. For nearly an hour, in her frail voice she shared stories about the Nazi's 900-day Siege of Leningrad.

FOR THE NEXT ten days, it was as if I'd never left. I taught lessons to many groups, engaged in provocative lunch conversations, took duty in the lobby in the early morning, played games in the hallway, and had conversations with Irina in her cabinet. I assisted Raisa Vladimirovna as she prepared her eighth-formers for their exam. I sat with parents in the lobby during exams and felt their tension; no one was allowed upstairs to observe. Later in the day, I photographed seventh-formers with their class teacher in Tavrichesky Park doing "socially useful work": raking leaves and preparing flower beds. And I attended a concert given by primary children for their parents. But I rarely laid eyes on Elvira.

At the Last Bell, she invited me to sit beside her on the stage. Sitting there, I felt her kindness. She must have been pleased that I had come. Otherwise, how could I have been in her school at all? Let alone able to teach the children again. And to attend the Last Bell, up front on the stage, to her right.

I watched the tenth-formers salute their teachers and the end of their lessons. Eyes welled up when a first-form girl in her brown uniform, starch-pressed white apron, with a giant chiffon bow atop her head walked slowly to Elvira's table, picked up the white ceramic bell and rang it to symbolize the last call for lessons. She set it down and rejoined her schoolmates to sing the haunting "*Do Svidaniya Schola*" ("Goodbye School"). In this Communist country with all of the Party's regulations and restrictions, a child is asked to lead one of its foremost ceremonies. So deeply felt. An expression of the collective, everyone invited in.

One by one the graduates recalled warm memories and presented flowers to their teachers; I, too, received red carnations. Near the end, Elvira invited me to speak. Having been given this opportunity, I chose to reflect on my walk with Nikolai and Roma, who had shared their obsession with Western clothes and goods.

"Love being Russian," I began. "Cherish your traditions. Nurture your lives and create your own future. The quick fix of foreign ways will only provoke frustration and disappointment. If you change, make the changes yourselves, make them in your own lives . . . ."

I concluded with a poem I had written with acknowledgement to Konstantin Simonov's "Wait for Me," which he wrote for his future wife, the well-known film and theater actress Valentina Serova.

My Russian Friends

Wait for us and we'll come back,
But wait with all your heart.
We need your waiting,
We need your patience.

Your struggle allows us time to catch up,
We who are ahead.
Invite us into your nests
And reach out to us.
Share with us your secret, your paradox
that friends come first,
despite a system that commands all to be no one,
except the one who is all.
Share with us your conscience
your memory of the horrors of war,
your soul that lures us to be with God.
Share with us your other secret
our future is knowing the past.
How else can we purge life from the precipice of holocaust?
It is you who may save us
Through your waiting.

Everyone smiled—few parents in the audience understood English—but gave a quiet, steady clap to show appreciation. In the Russian tradition, I clapped back.

A few days later, I left for home on the first day of June at four thirty in the morning, before the drawbridges reopened. I crossed the Liteyny Bridge in a taxi on my way to the airport. I had reveled with friends the night before to celebrate the beginning of the White Nights, days of summer where dusk meets dawn without night's intervention.

IV
ANGUISH AND SATISFACTION

Valéry Pavlovich was infamous for his concoctions of historical events—in line with falsifications in a society whose real history was being lost. Students became confused. Misha told me that when he was his student, it was impossible for adults to tell Valéry Pavlovich's stories from reality, let alone for Misha and his classmates.

Diary, October '87

Spies were indigenous to Soviet life. Elvira may have considered me one. In 1987, my second year as an exchange teacher in Leningrad, my colleague and I discovered that a KGB operative was living in our hotel. I think I saw him once. My phone lines hissed and moaned, probably a combination of Soviet technology and KGB wiretapping.

My suspicions were confirmed when Ludmilla Mikhailovna asked my colleague if he had enjoyed the wedding of an American rock singer to a Soviet bass player; he had told no one about it. Ludmilla then turned to me, raising her eyebrows, and, with a self-serving smirk, said, "Frank, you need to be careful if you choose to become involved with Russian women. You must be particularly careful having them in your room."

How did she know? And why did she know? But she obviously knew about my relationship with Elena Vladimovna, a teacher at School N° 185. It must have been from a tapped phone line, a listening device, or the KGB operative in the hotel. Most likely, the operative.

Elena, an English teacher, and I had become close. We'd met the year before, but she had shied away from forming a friendship. Attractive, with deep wide eyes, dark hair, and a quizzical smile, obviously melancholic, she was divorced—as I was—and lived with her mother and her young daughter. I often sensed her glancing my way, but she would turn away when I caught her eye. We scarcely spoke.

When I returned for my second teacher exchange, she made it a point to connect. She asked to meet after school at the Café Tarakan. In the course of our conversation, she expressed her deep respect for the way I treated students and other teachers. "You work to overcome evil with good," she said quietly. "I like the way you listen to us." Feeling her warmth, I invited her to my hotel room, the first of many frequent overnights as her mother would care for her daughter at home. She became another conduit—pun intended perhaps—an intimate one into learning about Soviet life.

When I shared with my close friend Misha Baushev Ludmilla's admonition of my behavior, his insightful manner tempered her comments. She was letting me know that others were aware of my activities, hinting that I should not do anything bad. A week later, another incident confirmed my suspicions about the KGB operative. My colleague's cleaning lady told an American student where he had gone to and when he would return.

Initially I felt offended that a KGB operative was spying on us—but not for long. If the KGB was spying on a couple of exchange teachers, either they must have been bored or had a serious underemployment issue. I could have tried to elude them, but that would have taken unnecessary energy. Choosing to use kopeks in pay phones or whispering on the phone in my room? What would I have been hiding?

And the presence of the KGB may have intimidated teachers or students from inviting me into their homes. I felt it strange at first not to be invited, except for the rare occasion. Irina's explanation when I asked her about it was that Russians were embarrassed, because of a lack of food, to have foreigners in their crowded quarters.

"Before a guest can come, they shop for hours, Frank," she said wearily, "for days perhaps, to find good food and drink. It takes preparation, you understand, if a family is to be ready to host you." I doubted that officials wanted this aspect of Soviet life to become common knowledge. Still, the Russians are a generous and hospitable people, which I discovered everywhere I went.

Even more curiously, a student told me that Elvira had admonished parents not to invite me unless they had respectable flats and her approval. Knowing that her husband was KGB may have deterred them further. Communal flats—several apartments sharing kitchen and bathroom facilities—were off limits. Elvira operated her school inside her cocoon, where we were free to mingle. Outside, we withdrew into our separate worlds: they to their flats, I to my hotel. Elvira would often invoke the Russian fear of foreigners, a fear embedded for hundreds of years beginning with the Mongol occupation in the thirteenth century. Gorbachev's efforts to alleviate that fear would take more time; nearly seven years would not be enough. The coming of Putin enshrined that fear.

When I returned as an AFS exchange teacher in a different school the following fall, I frequently rode buses back to School Nº 185. Because I was again there in an official capacity, Elvira resurrected our habit of having conversations in her cabinet. Her stories were gems, insightful, reflecting her conservatism. One afternoon, she railed (my cassette recorder in my pocket):

Morality is limping today! Perestroika! Even seven-year-olds
want it! We need to develop the culture of thinking. School
should be a proper school, practically. We should build moral-
ity before democracy!

Demonstrations! Such glasnost actions are against teach-
ers and workers. We got the crazy idea from the West and we
adopt it—like it is tacked on. It is better for people to work
than to protest. They are just lazy.

Elvira also seethed about her librarian who had an ill daughter
and took sick leave for the year. "She's worked here more than eight
years," she said, nearly shouting, "so now she can get a doctor's certificate of family leave, stay out for six months, and receive full pay!
She comes back for a day, practically—that word again—and then
gets another certificate." Quieting her voice, she added, "So I close
the library, lock it, and wait for her return."

I'd seen only one library, in October 1985, when Natasha
took me to her friend's small library at School N° 86. I never saw
another one. I imagined that other libraries would have been
much like it. Besides, what purpose would a library serve in a
school? What materials, other than government-produced books,
media, and its two newspapers, *Pravda* and *Izvestia*, would be
allowed? And given that the classroom was the focus of learning—and that the schedule was jam-packed—a library would
have been superfluous.

My own school had just been renovated around a library/media
center, which became a hub of activity throughout the day. Students
pursued books, audio-visual sources, research, and had access to
a plethora of publications. But why would a Soviet student have a
need to go to the library? The classroom curriculum was over-ex-
tended—deliberate on the part of Moscow; all textbooks and readers
were published from the capital. Much of the teaching centered on

reading, memorizing, and parroting those books, which was necessary for passing exams for university.

Soviet school libraries: an oxymoron if ever there was one.

Elvira and I had returned to our old groove. But I was aware, as always, that she might not be telling all. Were we continuing to play the part of a superficial relationship? Were both of us avoiding exploration of the deeper layers of Russian life? Was she talking about what *really* mattered? But when she told a story from her last visit to the States, her tone shifted, as if we were in another time, away from her having to pontificate as the matron of her domain. She spoke from the heart.

"I was sitting on a bus opposite a Negro [her term] mother and her seven kids. None of them offered an old woman a seat. We, who were over fifty, did!" Then in an almost-humble voice, she added, "I like your schools. We seemed to have lost the idea of 'this school is ours,' where yours seem to have much pride. You are very fortunate. We cannot seem to get any good changes in our schools anymore."

SHORTLY AFTER MY exchange, Valéry Pavlovich, a longtime history teacher, returned from a leave to be class advisor to the 8B form, which had some of my favorite students. One day, abruptly, without warning, Valéry told them, "Mr. Thoms, the exchange teacher who was here last fall, was an American spy. Whatever you think of him, he was first and foremost a spy."

I learned about Valéry's admonition to my former students while having coffee at the Café Tarakan with my friend and former lover, Elena Vladimovna. When Valéry moved on again to another school, she became 8B's class teacher. She was furious with his deceit.

"It's awful, Frank, when I heard him say that, playing with their minds like that! He's so cruel! I hope he rots in his new job!"

Valéry Pavlovich was infamous for his concoctions of historical events—in line with official falsifications in a society whose real history was being lost. Students became confused. Misha told me that when he was his student, it was impossible for adults to tell Valéry Pavlovich's stories from reality, let alone for Misha and his classmates. Because Valéry was a teacher in a one-party state, his word would not have not been challenged. Had Elena not confronted his deceit, my former students might still have believed him.

And had I not returned, I would never have known that a teacher would act as an informant, let alone inform on me. I could not imagine such a possibility, that a teacher would simply make up stories and inflict them on his unsuspecting students. But in a society that spawned its own versions of truth, Valéry Pavlovich was not an oxymoron.

Elena reestablished my good relationship with the class by arranging for me to give some lessons and attend a class party and a dance. She invited me to join a class trip to Lenfilm studios as long as I would not open my mouth, which would reveal that I was a foreigner. Because of my silence, our host looked confused and asked the students about me.

"He's our teacher," said Tanya. "He cannot hear because he's deaf."

"How then could he be your teacher?" the woman asked with a deep frown.

After some scrambling, and barely containing themselves, the kids avoided having me talk; they could have said I had laryngitis. After we left, everyone burst out laughing "like crazy, like crazy," my friend Katya told me years later. Without Russian fluency, I had no clue as to what they were saying. But living clandestinely was better than being ostracized.

In January 1991, passing through Leningrad to Alma-Ata, Kazakhstan, I planned to stop in at my beloved School N° 185. The night before, I had supper with my good friend Misha. In the course of our conversation, I told him of my intention to visit. He leaned back and folded his arms. After a pause, he said, "Elvira is angry with you, Frank, very angry. She heard from Illya, an émigré in New Hampshire, that you bad-mouthed her school in one of your talks. She's very upset."

I didn't know what to say. How could I have said anything bad about my favorite Leningrad school? It must have been at my talk at Portsmouth High School in front of more than one hundred students. I had no idea an émigré was in the hall, let alone Illya from School N° 185. What had I said? Had I shared that *shpora* (crib sheets) was endemic? Or that Soviet toilet paper never tore properly? That food shopping was difficult? Maybe examples of *pokazukha*? Whatever I said that day, I intended people to know of my respect for Russians and their struggle under Communism. I lauded my days at School N° 185 and the joy that I shared with Elvira, Irina, and everyone at the school.

Why had Elvira's former student, who had never met me, decided to tell her something negative? What did he have to gain? Perhaps he felt guilty about having left his homeland. His reporting would assuage his guilt. Whatever I'd said—or whatever he thought I'd said—it was enough for him, an incorruptible Soviet émigré, to report to Elvira. As Valéry Pavlovich had tried to break my trust with students, a former student had broken my trust with Elvira.

How was it possible to be in this situation again? Had I once again not been enough? I had never intended to offend anyone. Yet apparently, I had. Still, I would try to meet with her. As I entered her cabinet, she furrowed her brow, hardly looking at me, and in her high-pitched voice, she said, "Why have you said bad things about our school to Americans? Why you, Frank? Why?"

I tried to explain, but she had no interest in hearing me. I backed out of her cabinet feeling a deep sadness, taking in what would likely be my last look. Irina and some of the other teachers consoled me, but they could say nothing to her. Three months later, on my way home from Alma-Ata, I again tried to see her. Still no change of heart. In her eyes, I had failed to be part of the collective. Perhaps I should have been more low-key when sharing my impressions. Russians keep what they know close to the chest. I, on the other hand, prefer to share what I discover, what I learn. I was proud to have been in School N⁰ 185 and wanted everyone to know it.

In the end, all the hours Elvira and I had spent together were not enough for me to belong. She had closed the door—forever. I'd broken the covenant of the collective, that part of the *matryoshka* that does not allow room for individual expression, no room for revealing its inner workings. I missed our relationship. I missed the apparent trust we'd formed, but a trust it was not, not after she felt I had violated it.

No matter how hard we try to become immersed inside another culture, we remain on the outside. Sometimes we think we are inside, but it is tenuous at best. When it's the culture of "the enemy," the challenge is doubly difficult.

WHEN I WAS in Leningrad for the last time in 1994, I spoke with Katya Shrayber, who'd been one of my favorite eighth-formers at School N⁰ 185. She offered a fresh perspective. "Before Gorbachev's ascension, the school had hosted more foreign delegations than any other in the city," Katya said. "After the end of Communism, Elvira kept the school connected to foreigners and continued to have AFS exchange teachers.

"She is not a black-and-white woman, you know, Frank. Elvira understood what it meant to have a good education, and she attracted good teachers. Despite the tenor of anti-Semitism in Russia, she hired Jews like Raisa Vladimirovna." Katya then spoke of how industry was failing in the new Russia, and traditional factory support for school had declined. Elvira, in her cleverness, found new sponsors to support school programs—Russia's newly rich businessmen.

"These businessmen send their children to the school, Frank. Each of them pays tuition as a sponsor (five million rubles, $2,500) to get their children into the school. Elvira now has money for excursions and special events. The daughters of the mayor of the city and of the American Consul attend the school. And the school has become known as the school where children go abroad.

"In 1989, when a former student was running for mayor of Leningrad on a progressive platform," Katya added, "Elvira purged the school of all posters and banners depicting Lenin and replaced them with them with images of Tolstoy, Dostoyevsky, and others. She always seemed to know where her butter was spread."

What a move, Elvira, I thought. You, the majordomo of your domain, have maintained your privileged status in the new Russia. Like when you ordered students not to wear foreign pins on their uniforms to impress an inspector, you never hesitated to act on the "right side." And you tore down the Lenin posters before the fall of Communism. Quite the chutzpah!

Vivacious, curious, and confident, Katya emigrated to the US in 1997 and is now married and working for a pharmaceutical company in California. We reunited in June 2018 in Mill Valley after nearly thirty years. Over coffee and pastries at a café, in her gentle Slavic-accented English she told the story about the olive-green jacket that I wore every day when teaching in her school.

> *Every day you came to our school in Green Jacket with brown patches on the elbows. It was like a symbol of a free world. All the other teachers wore boring gray and blue clothing. I wrote in my diary, which I found recently: 'Today we had an American teacher, Frank Thoms, come to our school, who is wearing a green jacket. He's completely different from our other teachers. He looks like a movie star.' And, Frank, you*

brought food into the classroom, which no other teacher did. Sometimes, you brought compote and pastry from the cafeteria.

The last time I saw you in Leningrad was when we met at a railway station where we were seeing off a friend of ours. You'd heard from Misha Baushev that we were getting together there. After meeting at the railway station, you and Misha went with us to another friend's house. We reminisced about our great times. It was then when I first told you about Green Jacket. For you it was just a green jacket, but for us, when we first saw you back in October 1986, it was part of a different world. Later, at the railway station, when you were leaving for Moscow, you took off the jacket and gave it to me and asked that we remember you.

In the years that followed in Russia, many people I knew were emigrating; there was a huge brain drain among my friends. In 1997, when I emigrated to the US, Green Jacket became a symbol that we would someday reunite. Everyone knew I had Green Jacket. When I was leaving, I was not able to take it with me, but I asked my mom to keep it, as this was a tie that connected me to my childhood and to the memories that I cherished. In 2002, when I visited my parents in Saint Petersburg, I asked my mom about Green Jacket, but she said that, unfortunately, it had been ruined by moths. I was very upset as this was more than a jacket to me; it was a symbol.

But, Frank, you won't believe it, the story of Green Jacket is still alive, at least in our hearts. When I first found you on the internet many years later through Facebook, I wrote a post: 'Do you remember green jacket?' 'Of course I remember green jacket,' they said and told stories about you. So Green Jacket is still alive. All my classmates remember you. Green

*Jacket has had a purpose, Frank, a great purpose. You made
a big impact on us.*

In 2016, I learned that Elvira Nikolaevna and Irina Nikolaevna had died. Hard to believe, as I still hold these two schoolmarms in my mind, two devoted educators, each having her own persona. Each in her own way invited me into her *matryoshka*. We'd met at a time when Gorbachev's Soviet Union was reaching out to America and reaching into itself. Irina was Irina, no doubt the same Irina before Gorbachev and after. Elvira, the good Communist, became the clever entrepreneur in the new Russia. And she would have fit right into Putin's regime. After all, her husband had been KGB.

V
TEACHERS AS MOTHERS OF THE STATE

"I am like a mother to them, the bábushka *who sees no wrong in her grandchildren. I am their advocate in the system."*

Zoya Anatolyevna, Nov. '86

Boarding the Red Arrow Express at Leningrad's Moskovskaya station, I bade farewell to Irina Nikolaevna—one of the first to welcome me, the last to say goodbye. For my final days, I wanted to linger in Peter's serf-built city, constructed on a swamp; to stroll along its canals, walk its wide streets, and observe its elegant architecture leaning toward Europe. Would I come back?

I've been twice to Moscow, an unwieldy, dirty, impersonal city, dotted with Stalin's seven aberrant, Gothic, wedding-cake buildings. But it had Red Square, St. Basil's, the Kremlin. I often stared at the repetitive changing of the guard at Lenin's Mausoleum, marveling at its precision.

The mausoleum, a stunted, rose-hued, marble pyramid, had been inserted into Red Square's regal history by an upstart Party fearful of its people. On the hour, two soldiers and an escort in army-green uniforms, cylindrical military hats, gold lanyards, and waist belts hold upright bayoneted rifles as they goose-step toward the entrance of the crypt housing the preserved Lenin-God lying below in a crystal casket. Upon arrival, in a flick of an instant, the two soldiers replace their comrades, stand on red square carpets facing each other—erect, rigid, still.

Every hour: Step! Step! Step! Step! In time with the heartbeat of a dead man.

When my exchange-teacher colleagues and I arrived from Leningrad, I immediately appealed to our host, Yevgeny, a calm bureaucrat, to allow me to visit another school rather than take another tour of the city. He asked his assistant, the perky Yana, to bring me to School № 21. I would have two more days in a Soviet school. Would it be like School № 185? Would the director even let me in? If so, would I be able to teach?

After entering the building, Yana took me to a primary class where I received the foreign-visitor treatment. The pupils stood in unison, and the teacher gestured for me to sit in the back. Like teachers I had observed in Leningrad, she evoked the stand-up, sit-down lesson of the Great Teacher in the Soviet sky, discharging Soviet curricula, plying repetitive Soviet methodology with Soviet textbooks in front of her Young Oktobrists, sitting straight in pairs before her. Her classroom was used to hosting foreigners.

Later in the morning, Yana left without introducing me to the director. I wandered up to the second floor. I paused and looked into a room where students were jousting and laughing—and a girl was playing a piano. A tall young woman saw me and approached from across the room. I still see her with her pulled-back brown hair, blue sneakers, white rolled socks, stooped shoulders—having been a tall, shy schoolgirl—twinkling eyes peering through pink-tinted myopic spectacles with ornate temples. She grinned as she limply shook my hand.

"Good morning," she said in a soft voice barely rising above the bedlam, "I'm Zoya Anatolyevna. Will you teach my children?" Just like that. No assessment of who I was. Or asking why I was there.

"What's the lesson today?"

"You don't prefer to talk with them?"

"I'd prefer for the first time to teach from the text. Which lesson are you on?"

I had become tired of talking about America. I preferred to mingle with the makings of their lives, their daily fare. Teaching from the text created an immediate bond. Lessons in all schools had become a national shared memory; mention "The Black Cat" or "What Is More Useful," and every special-English-language student remembers. Begin reciting a Pushkin poem, and the Russians in the room—or on a bus, as happened to me in New York—recite it with you.

Zoya's welcome let me know that we would find common ground. I thought about having her students address me with what would have been my Russian patronymic, the way students referred to their teachers and director: Raisa Vladimirovna, Zoya Anatolyevna, Elvira Nikolaevna, Victor Vladimirovich, et al. But in Leningrad when I tried "Frank Frankovich" (my first name plus my father's name), the sound of that name made students laugh. Sometimes I would miss having them use my patronymic. I settled for "Mr. Thoms" or "Mr. Frank."

"Today's lesson, Frank, is number four, 'Karl Marx.' Take a look at it while I talk with them about some class business."

My first chance to teach Marx to Soviets! I read the lesson and noted its one-sided stance, its imbalance, loaded with praise for the forebear of Communism. I seized on the last paragraph: "Marx was the best-hated man of the century, but also the best loved. The best-hated by the oppressors and exploiters, the best-loved by the oppressed and exploited."

I began the lesson in my usual manner, asking for names and writing them down in relation to where they sat. I wanted to remember as many of them as I could, because Zoya had already expressed her interest in having me back the next day. Scanning the room, I sensed a restlessness. Not all were in uniforms. They sat scattered about, not in pairs at desks. I decided to skip the usual retelling of the text; I would ask the five questions that I'd prepared.

Who does Marx describe as the oppressors and the oppressed?

Who are the exploiters and the exploited?

If the oppressors are capitalists, why are people in capitalist societies richer than people in socialist societies?

Are there oppressed people in socialist societies?

Are there oppressed peoples in the Soviet Union?

I asked the first question and the room came alive. Several began to speak at the same time. No one raised his hand. No one waited for my permission to proceed. The conversation became argumentative at times but with an obvious respect for one another—and for me. Zoya, on a stool by the piano in the back of the room, her long legs crossed, was smiling. (I wished I'd had my cassette recorder on.)

It was almost as if I were in my classroom back home. I wondered if Moscow schools, which were closer to the country's shifting mood toward Gorbachev's *glasnost*, were relaxing their standards. Toward the end of the lesson, we discussed Marx's dialectical process. The students were challenged, often confused, perhaps from my delivery. I was pushing their thinking. The bell rang. No one stood to leave. They persisted with their questions and comments.

Over these two days, Zoya's eighth-formers and I became close like strangers on a plane. We spilled our minds to one another. They were free to be frank with the American. Was this happening because of Gorbachev? I wondered. Would another teacher in Zoya's school allow me to teach this way? Would these students have engaged like this if I had come during the Brezhnev era, which had preceded Gorbachev?

I imagined that, during Brezhnev's long reign, all the students would have been dressed in their blue or brown uniforms with red scarves sitting in pairs at tables, the flimsy-papered, Soviet English-language textbooks before them. They would have raised their right hand at the elbow and stood to speak in front of tired blackboards and crumbling chalk. Had I been invited to teach, I would likely have been forced to stick to the text. I doubt we would have been able to suspend our mutual disbelief and supersede our separate histories, separate systems, and separate purposes—even for one lesson. We would have remained in front of the red veil.

"You teach them to think, Frank," Zoya told me, taking my arm as we headed to the canteen for a cup of tea. "I really like the way you have them speak their minds."

"And I'm grateful, Zoya, that you have allowed me to teach the way I prefer. When students retell texts, they stand up one at a time, say what the text has told them, and sit down. That happens over and over. No back-and-forth. It leads to dead-end learning. I imagine you feel the same way."

"Yes, I do," she said in her calm, quiet voice. "But I am not always able to do what you did with my students. They have to prepare for exams in order to get into university. They need to know lots of information. But I keep the lessons as informal as I can. You know, Frank, I've been their class teacher—class tutor—for five years. We are very close. At breaks, they swarm into my room, spill their problems, and seek my advice. When those on duty come after school, they talk with me while pretending to mop the floor and wash the blackboard."

"I'm not surprised. They obviously respect and love you."

A YEAR LATER, I returned to Zoya's classroom. We talked about her role as a class tutor, her favorite part of her job: taking students on camping trips to the Baltic States, ski trips to the Carpathian Mountains, and tours to Leningrad. They would stay at her home when their parents were away or were having difficulties. And she cited her numerous burdensome school duties: organizing the Class Record Book, having to copy and recopy all forty names four times a year; collecting lunch money; assigning student monitoring posts; wearing a red armband when on duty—which she never did—all this while having to teach. Far more duties than I ever had.

In a country laden with authority, she and her colleagues had chutzpah. "You smoke in school?" I asked over tea. "Isn't it prohibited?"

"Yes, we are bad," Zoya said with a big grin. "Every day, I skip hall duty and smoke in the chem lab. Our director chastises us, but we do it anyway."

They weren't the only Russians I observed showing disrespect for the system. Once, during dinner with a friend in a Leningrad restaurant, a waitress asked him to put out his cigarette. He indicated that he would and continued to smoke for the rest of the meal. Nothing more was said. Another time in Kiev, the maître-d'hôtel insisted that my acquaintance and I not wear jeans in his restaurant. After some discussion, we proceeded upstairs to the dining room. Again, nothing more was said. It was the same when Elvira Nikolaevna asserted that students could no longer display lapel pins, so they pinned them underneath. Appearances were more important than substance— Soviet *pokazukha*.

I could not imagine my American friends and me carrying on any of these acts of defiance at home. All of them, from Zoya's smoking to Elvira's students wearing pins under their lapels, were done without fear of repercussion. But in the States, we are expected to comply when confronted for our misbehaviors. We might try to stretch the rules, but once caught in the act, we will most likely suffer consequences. In attempting to comprehend these Soviet behaviors, some American visitors may have been baffled, rationalized these instances with Churchill's "Russia is a riddle wrapped inside an enigma," and left it at that. As for me, I saw these cosmetic rebukes of defiant behaviors as *pokazukha*—efforts to prop up the red veil for outsiders to see.

ZOYA BECAME ENTWINED with the lives of her students. An egregious example concerned Illya, one of her favorites.

"Illya received a two [D] on his Russian exam last year, Frank, which meant he would be kept back in the eighth form. When he wrote his make-up exam, there were too many mistakes. He left out dashes, punctuation marks, capital letters, and other such things. So I asked the director to give me Illya's exam. I wanted to just look at it. I took my pen and put in the dashes and commas where necessary. Then I said to her, 'See there aren't many mistakes, so we can give him a three, not a two.' That's why he's with me in the ninth form now."

The director had looked through her fingers and said nothing.

"That's class-A *shpora*!"

Zoya looked at me and laughed. "I did it because he is lazy and only interested in certain subjects—and he works hard at them. If he doesn't like, he doesn't work; that's when he gets bad marks. He's a very clever boy. I could not bear to be without Illya. He has been with me since his second year. He is part of my family."

Curious that Zoya was able to improve Illya's exam score to a passing grade simply by correcting his punctuation. It made me wonder what the Soviet curriculum expected from students. Was the appearance of the exam, for example, more important than the content? Was following the rules of grammar enough? Did the appearance of success in this exam indicate another *pokazukha* in the Soviet lexicon?

"All Soviet teachers have the responsibility to care for everyone," she said emphatically. "As much as they may not like a child—or even his family—he's still in the form's family. As a class tutor, I work in a collective where everyone is responsible for everyone else. It can't be any other way."

Had I not been steeped in Soviet school culture, I might have challenged Zoya's behavior, perhaps engaged in an argument. But when in another culture, we can choose to step back and recognize that we are inside another way of life, another paradigm even. We allow ourselves to withhold judgment, to see the situation for what it is, to see from the other person's point of view. In this instance, Zoya was confronting Moscow's curriculum, which was, by design, overwhelming. It expected teachers and students to succumb to its demands. But by helping Illya, she was giving him room to grow. She was being a teacher, not a tool of the State. The best we can do is to imagine ourselves as observers from a bridge between two cultures, knowing that there is good and bad in each.

My efforts to connect with students was no match for Zoya's. As class teacher, not only did she take a deep personal interest in all her children, but she integrated them into the mores of Soviet society, nurtured their collective spirit, and inculcated purported Soviet values of honesty, integrity, cooperation, respect for others—and cheating when necessary. "I am like a mother to them, the *bábushka* who sees no wrong in her grandchildren. I am their advocate in the system." Zoya Anatolyevna reflected Soviet society itself, its womb-to-tomb, care-package upbringing. She was the quintessential class teacher.

The collective. So essential, it lived everywhere. I first understood the embedded collective mindset the day I followed an eighth-form class group at School N⁰ 185. Olya, my spindly friend from Raisa Vladimirovna's class, acted as my guide. After geography, we headed to the science room. By the time the bell rang, only Olya and three of her friends had arrived. The rest were nowhere to be found. Ten minutes before the end of the period, they straggled in, slumped into their seats with red faces, shortened breath, and wide eyes.

"Where have you been?" I asked Gleb; I knew him from Raisa's class.

He took a breath. "We've been outside playing frozen tag. We went across the street where nobody could find us." Short, spunky, and clever, I figured Gleb to be the leader.

"So, you are the one who decided to skip science class."

"Oh no, not me. We all decided."

I pressed him but to no avail.

At the beginning of the next period, Irina Nikolaevna stormed into the room and expressed her indignation at their misbehavior. Nothing more happened. Skipping science had been a collective decision. No need for her or Elvira to seek the perpetrator. Later, reflecting on Gleb's intransigent stance, I understood that he and his classmates had made the decision together. They had grown up in a collective.

The collective is a cocoon, one that protects each member. Irina could only chastise. She did not try to single out a perpetrator—as I attempted to with Gleb. It had been a collective decision. If a punishment had been warranted, she would have exacted one. But science was over. The next class was about to begin. And to consider putting them in after-school detention? Not possible, not even a thought. Absurd, in fact. All members of the form would have to be there. Two forms on the same day would mean they would have to be placed in the assembly hall. No teachers would want to have to supervise that! Besides, they needed to go home after school to take care of their families.

When we observe collective behavior, we can be taken in by its inclusiveness. Everyone acts as if they belong. In the US, focus on the individual tends to make people wary of one another. Even on the same team, players sometimes feel competitive with teammates. The collective behavior I observed supported its members, but it also hindered. It forced everyone to be on the same page. To deviate would be to defy the group. To become exceptional would mean to separate oneself. And if one were weak, he would need to be propped up. The collective needed to appear as one for every member, as one for the school, and as one for the State. It would take considerable courage to defy the collective.

OCTOBER 1988: My third and last time with Zoya and her tenth form. She asked me to teach one more class. Olya, one of the most outspoken students the last time we met, sprawled her lanky sixteen-year-old self at her desk in the back, her wispy, light brown hair flailing behind, her slender hands fidgeting with her pen, her papers, and her hair. She wanted more than she ought to ask for—and she asked anyway. She expected much from her classmates, more than most of them understood. She took up a lot of personal space like an American, and unlike most of her peers, who shared space with one another interlocking arms or resting a hand on a friend's shoulder.

Flaunting her disdain for the school uniform, she wore whatever she could find from the West—anything not Soviet. On this day, she had a light blue sweater with oversized shoulder pads. Her ideas drew more attention than her appearance or personality. During discussions, she thrust ideas onto her classmates, pummeled them with her passionate beliefs. Before I could ask the class for their perceptions of democracy, Olya—not unexpectedly—blurted out (this time, my cassette recorder on):

"The school is a little world! Sometimes when things are done in the Party or society, it doesn't touch the schools. For example, we now have *glasnost*—and I cannot say what I think! I can say what I want to the director, but I will suffer consequences, problems. It can have consequences on my characteristics [teacher recommendations]. This forces me not to say anything!"

"Where is democracy in this school?" I inquired.

Ira, usually quiet, thoughtful but forceful, sat up. "The level of democracy depends upon the teacher, teachers who do not depend on the director. It exists in Boris London's literature class. We can say what we want to say. Democracy, to me, means this freedom to speak, the right of all pupils to say what they want to say."

"But it is a fragile democracy," cried out an animated Olya, "when it depends on the teacher in class or Gorbachev who allows it in the Party."

I put two concepts on the board: "democracy by permission" and "grassroots democracy." Hoping to enrich the conversation, I sat down to listen.

"Democracy is just another stage of society," said Aysa, dressed in her proper uniform and well respected. "All the citizens must come upon this idea from within. They must be free among themselves. No one can give it to them."

Marina, one of the talkers the last time we met, said, "The Soviet Union is not ready for democracy. People need more time. I need more time."

From the back of the room in a quiet voice, Dima, dark-haired and pensive, said, "Democracy is freedom in your soul."

Practically jumping out of her seat, again Olya spoke up. "If I have nothing to say, what will be the democracy? It will be just words. If I have nothing to fight about, nothing to change, if I don't know what to change, if I don't know what to do, I do not have any democracy. If I don't have anything in me, what to say, I don't need democracy!"

The conversation continued for another half hour. The intensity brought out more Russian mixed with English—somewhat difficult for me but good for them. The debate continued as ideas germinated. I wondered how my presence affected what they were saying. Was my being an American giving them room to speak freely? Or had Zoya already set that tone? She sat in the back frequently grinning, her long legs crossed and bouncing, exposing her rolled-up white socks and sneakers.

Olya's last flourish was, "Mr. Frank, don't you think that our foundation isn't democratic when there is only one party in the society? Why do I hear all day long, 'Marx and Lenin,' 'Communist Party,' 'Communist Party,' 'Communist Party' all day long! What about 'Fascist Party'? Why can't I even look at their materials?"

Olya was a child of *glasnost*, a spokesperson for a possible future, yet at the same time an aberration, ahead of the realities of the present.

The bell rang. Again, nobody got up to leave. I stood up. "I will defect and come to help you learn about other parties. I will help you make your revolution." Chuckles, grins . . . . We agreed to agree that democracy includes obligations as well as rights.

And Ira, who had spoken well of Boris London's literature class, offered the last word: "Gorbachev and democracy do not mix. Now we have a problem. Our constitution has lost its importance. It needs to be changed." How prescient!

As I listened to Zoya's cherubs, I felt I was witnessing a private conversation, one not meant for foreigners. I was inside a part of the *matryoshka* where perhaps I should not have been. These students led me to move away from my teacher-ego, the front-and-center person who would run the show. I sat back; my presence more than enough. And the conversation may only have happened because I *was* there. I was hearing from the core of these students.

I thought about my students at home. How could I engage them to wrestle with our democracy? To think critically about what works? Assess whom our democracy benefits the most? As I was listening, I realized that most Americans were complacent about their government. We were the world's leading democracy. I wanted to return home and tell teachers, who were tied to stringent curriculums, to let go and open up to listening to their students, to ferret out the Olyas waiting to be heard.

Zoya's students were energized by *glasnost*, but where would it take them? Thirty years later as I write these words, I wonder what those then-young people are now thinking. And in America today, given the deep political divide, I hope teachers will choose to emulate

Zoya Anatolyevna's classroom and provide opportunities for students to wrestle freely with issues.

EACH TIME I returned to Zoya's second-floor room, it was as if we'd been put on pause, only to restart when we gathered again. I did not come as an exchange teacher to fulfill expectations under the guise of authority. I slipped through the cracks of officialdom—I never saw the director. I was "Mr. Frank" who listened to the voices of young Soviets, entered their hearts, as they entered mine, their American friend.

I came from a country they knew from the newspapers *Pravda* and *Izvestia*, and *Vremya* State television, from textbooks and political information classes. They read about Wall Street, skyscrapers, and about unemployed homeless wrapped in cardboard lying on grates in the winter's cold. There was no middle ground. I saw myself as that middle ground—a bridge—where they could discover about America from an American who listened to them; they could digest his words for themselves.

I wondered if the boring nature of the Soviet curriculum and propaganda aided my efforts to spark their thinking. Except for Russian literature with Boris London—as Ira had intimated in our first conversation—and with Zoya, their empathetic class teacher, these Soviet students were not free to speak their mind. They had to chase a curriculum that eluded them, that was impossible to master. They had to retell one lesson after another, after another, after another . . . with no time for speculation. And in nearly all those lessons, they had to stand to speak, which left no opportunity for conversation. I offered relief from that tediousness, the repetitive boredom inculcating Soviet patriotism.

BEFORE I LEFT Zoya and her tenth-formers for the last time in the fall of 1988, I asked her how she would feel when they graduated the next spring.

"I'll still see them on special days," she said with a big grin. "We have some good traditions. We will celebrate the birthday of our class with their parents at a special concert on the first Saturday in November. Also, on the first Sunday in September, we will go on a picnic as we always have. On the first day of school, they will come to see me. And on the twelfth of December, they will celebrate my birthday."

Her class would always be hers, a possessiveness far in excess of any I've felt. Each year that I had with a class, I came to see them as my own. I become possessive, more than I let on. I did not see myself as their father or surrogate parent, but as an adult who cared about each one of them. But Zoya had been their mother, their *bábushka* for five years. Letting go of them was the farthest thought in her mind. Her collective would remain embedded well beyond its designated time. After a year off, she would have another class, a beginning of another five years as their mother.

But she never organized a new family. In the summer of 1990, she left Moscow, left the Soviet Union forever. In a letter to me written in March, she wrote:

I am sure you have heard about the situation in our country. It's horrible. The state of affairs in many parts of this country can be characterized as real war. We have many difficulties in every field of our life. Now we are afraid for our children's future. We are afraid we will lose our friends, parents, children. I feel I can do nothing for my country in this case.

Zoya was scared, scared for herself, her daughter, and her friends. She saw her country slipping into chaos, her way of life threatened, especially her life as a teacher. Like a dog who could feel the coming of an earthquake, Zoya sensed, I believe, that Communism would soon unravel. What that would entail was anybody's guess. Maybe, too, her fears may have stemmed from being Jewish—I didn't know. Some of my Jewish friends in Leningrad had shared hints of a possible pogrom. I couldn't think of other reasons Zoya would want to leave the country. I wish I'd asked her more questions about her life.

Zoya revealed a side of herself she had not shared. In the conclusion of that same March letter, she wrote in hopes that I could send her an invitation to come to live in America.

> *I have many questions. You are the only person who can help me find answers, Frankusha [a nickname she and others had given me]. I don't want to do you any harm, but you are the only person I trust. If the hole [sic] idea is not crazy, please write if you can send us the invitation. I hope to hear from you soon. Each day means so much for us now. My love to you.*

I had no means to invite her. I recalled Elvira and Irina's powerlessness to invite me back to School № 185. I replied to Zoya:

> *As for helping you to come here to live, I am very limited. For example, if I were to invite you, I would have to be responsible for your health care and your living until you could make it on your own. I am still writing full time and do not have a job yet . . . .*
>
> *I am suspended between two realities: my heart cries out to reach out and snatch you and Sasha, André, and Grisha, and to bring you here; and the other reality, the knowledge that I cannot. You all are in my heart. Please do not despair. May you find peace in your days of turmoil, peace in your hearts, and hope for the future.*

Her next letter arrived in June.

Dear Frankusha, I write to you from Stockholm. We (Sasha, André, and I) are here now. The situation in our country became even worse, so we have moved to Sweden. We come on the invitation of friends. We now are living in a hotel for émigrés from different countries. Our plans are to stay here. I hope it will be better for Sasha here, but we always think about our relations in Moscow, about our country.

She must have become desperate. She couldn't wait for a possible invitation from me. In fact, her mother told her that letters from me had come to her Moscow address, but she'd already left.

In the fall, she wrote another letter. After describing her new life in Sweden and hopes for a work permit, she said:

Frankusha dear, you can't imagine how I miss my parents, my dear kids from School Nº 21, my friend Grisha from Moscow, and of course you. Dear Zaichik Frankusha, even now I feel confusion . . . . It was selfish to shift my difficulties on you, but I hope you can understand me. Your letters helped me, all of us at that moment.

I don't know if we will stay in Sweden or not, but I hope to see you, to hear from you as soon as possible. Please don't forget me. I think I live with all the difficulties because you remember us. I love you, best wishes to you. God bless you! Please keep us in your heart.

I did. Nearly thirty years later, I still think about her. In her last letter, she wrote that she, André, and Sasha had moved to Gimo, two hours north of Stockholm. And in that letter, she expressed deep concern for her Russia after the fall of Gorbachev.

You know, Frankusha, sometimes I want to be on a desert island to know nothing, to hear nothing about these terrible things, but we live on the same planet and these problems are ours. The only thing we can do is to love each other, to help each other, to be kind.

And at the end:

You know, I am waiting for a second child. Sasha and André are waiting for a boy, but I am happy that in May I'll have a baby.

Zoya seemed to be settling into her new life in Sweden. Perhaps she found a teaching position and could pursue her devotion to her children, her gift of empathy for the young. And were she in Moscow today, she might well be terrified. She had seen her students becoming outspoken and open. She wanted them to have the freedom that she had come to know through them. Her Olya, in Western dress lamenting the lack of democracy, spoke for the inner Zoya, whose smiles from the back of the room let me know that. But the Russia they were hoping for has not materialized.

We have lost contact. As happens in our lives, we meet people who become important to us, but alas, we fade into each other's woodwork. Her life focused on her new country, mine on a return to matters at home. I did mail a letter this year to her last address in Gimo, Sweden, but to no avail; it was returned a month later.

JUNE, 1987: I'd been in the Soviet Union three times, each trip more revealing. I'd spent twenty-five years in the classroom, returning periodically to explore Marxist socialism, Russian history, Communism, and the Soviet Union. If I were to pursue my obsession to investigate behind the red veil, I would have to leave my middle-school teaching position, its guaranteed contract, and its familiar community. I decided one afternoon to let it all go and resign. For the first time in twenty-five years, I would let go of the security blanket of "being a teacher," the public veil that had become my identity. I'd come close to the Russian people. I'd seen enough to begin writing a book. I wanted to discover my understanding of this mysterious culture. A new Communism seemed to be emerging, and I had been a witness. I needed time.

I left the superintendent's office that day with only a small savings account, no contract, no job in reserve, no place to live, no guarantees of any kind. But I stepped into the bright sunny afternoon three feet off the ground. A sense of freedom, a new world full of possibilities awaited me. Divorced, my two children grown, I would be the agent of my own destiny.

The following Sunday at the Society of Friends meeting, where I'd been a member for nearly ten years, I announced my decision. Words rolled off my tongue without hesitation; I was committed to write about my teaching and living in the Soviet Union. After meeting, two members approached me and offered me a bedroom in their homes, "in exchange for doing a few chores." Two weeks later I was sitting before my Macintosh at a large oak desk in a spacious upstairs room with a single bed in the far corner of a colonial farmhouse looking out onto the broad hillsides of Meriden, New Hampshire.

For six months, I tapped on my Macintosh keyboard with my index fingers. I transcribed nearly one hundred hours of tapes I'd recorded on my Olympus mini-cassette recorder—mostly from my pocket. Hearing the voices of friends and acquaintances, I relived those moments, remembering where we were. I was immersing myself more deeply in the Soviet *matryoshka*, becoming more intimate with the Russian psyche.

Every day, I wrote. Elvira and Irina would sit in front of me sometimes. And so would Vika, Julia, Dima, Alyosha, and a host of other students. I relived School N° 185's bustling hallways, my lively lessons in English, and the farewell concert. And the sights and smells of the streets of Leningrad, Natasha in her flat in Petrogradskaya, and Alexei and Román and the girls. And Moscow's Red Square, and Zoya, Olya, and the eighth form at School N° 21. My middle school classroom, its twenty-five wonderful years, began to fade. I had no regrets. I was anticipating a new future.

For the first time in my life, I was beholden to no one. No job. No family. No relationship. Just me and my Macintosh. And I was in the presence of two dear Quakers, Japanese-Americans, Mayme and Lafayette Noda, who invited me to their table for meals. Mayme was a firecracker. Her conversations, cooking, and housekeeping withal embodied flair. Lafayette, professor emeritus of biochemistry at Dartmouth Medical School, was contemplative, caring for his blueberry and Christmas tree farms and meditating every day. Over the next year and a half as I pursued my writing, I became a member of the family. Mayme's work ethic inspired me to stay with my writing every day. Lafayette's tranquility led me to look inside myself. One morning after breakfast, I returned to my room and wrote:

As I came downstairs for breakfast this morning in my New Hampshire kitchen on a cold January morning, I felt the frost creeping through its walls. I lit the woodstove. The frost edged away, and warmth replaced cold. I pondered exchanges: light greeting dark at dawn, warm air meeting ice, waves transposing rocks into sand.

Life is a process of exchanging. At birth we exchange the womb for the outside world. At death we leave for wherever. Life invites us to become active at the edges, where new ideas touch the old, where the strange confronts the familiar, where crises infringe on quiet.

As the kitchen warmed, I reflected on my trips to

Leningrad. Being in a foreign culture—especially in the cul-
ture of "the enemy"—stimulates me. At home, I maintain rou-
tines, live inside my culture. In Leningrad, my visa is finite;
I'm a foreigner watched by the KGB.

I remembered my first time in Peter's great city. Nina, our
tour guide, spoke about its origins and pointed to its monu-
ments. I longed to get off the Intourist bus and walk its back
streets, to look into the eyes of its people. The night of our
arrival at the airport, I met Natasha and her two children.
Two days later I was having lunch in her flat.

Returning, I slip deeper into its culture, closer to its
people, less confident about what I know. Exchanges become
less abrupt, less instant, more subtle, more lingering. We find
moments to share the same perspective.

I was ready for the next stage in seeking to know Russians behind
the red veil.

Later in the summer, a most unexpected letter arrived from AFS.
They invited me to be included in the next exchange teacher program, again in Leningrad! As much as it was a surprise—as far as I
knew, no one had gone twice—it also felt natural. I was destined to
be with Russians, what Zoya once called my second country. Again I
would spend three months in my favorite city. A chance to be on my
own behind the red veil. And I would have new material for my book.

Arrangements for this teacher exchange went smoothly. Two days
after flying into Moscow, I again arrived on the Red Arrow Express
to Leningrad's Moskovsky Station and to Ludmilla Mikhailovna and
her committee's curt welcome. No Victor Vladimirovich, no Irina
Nikolaevna, no School N° 185. Instead, Ludmilla placed me in School
N° 169, an unexpected detour into a time before Gorbachev.

VI
THE CULT OF LENIN

"I implore you, then, to step off Moscow's curriculum train and take time to listen to your students. You will be better for it. Each child is a drop of rain. Cherish each drop, love each drop. You should not simply listen to the storm."

My speech to Leningrad's English Teachers, November '87

Haven't these people even heard of Mikhail Gorbachev? Are they still living in the Brezhnev era with its strict Communist protocols? Or even in the time of Lenin and Stalin? I asked myself these questions as I left School N⁰ 169 after my initial meeting with its director, Rima Alexandrovna and English department head, Valentina Valentinovna. I'd been tossed back into a time before *glasnost*, before anyone acknowledged Communism's uncertain future. I recalled the anecdote of the boy whose parents sent him to different schools without success. Each time he was dismissed, until at a Catholic school he became a serious student. When his parents asked him why, he said, "They mean business. You should see what they do to those who don't obey. They nail them to a cross!"

At School N⁰ 169, it was Lenin. When I stepped into its front vestibule, there was a life-sized, white bronze statue of the man-god leaning forward on a low pedestal, holding his workman's cap in his right hand which rested on his thigh, his left hand wrapped around the back a young boy sporting a spiked foot-soldier's helmet. Lenin's eyes gazed on a smaller barefoot boy to his right wearing a similar workman's cap, and a third boy sat below in front with adoring eyes. Light from a nearby window highlighted the deep red backdrop. It was clear that disobedience to the father of the Soviet Union was not an option.

The next door led into a spacious lobby. Six Young Pioneers, some with bowed heads, stood to greet me in front of bulletin boards displaying large red posters depicting Marxian sagacity and Lenin aphorisms. Valentina Valentinovna, whom I'd met at the railway station, stood to one side waiting to take me to the director. She was young for a department head, well-dressed in her smart dark-rose-colored suit, and having short, curled, light brown hair, a clear complexion, and a reserved smile revealing slightly spaced front teeth. A soft voice, large brown eyes, her manner formal—and detached.

She led me into a spacious cabinet. At the far end stood the director, Rima Alexandrovna, hardly taller than the back of her chair, extending her hand across her oversized wooden desk. Her eyes were magnified through prodigious plastic-rimmed spectacles set on her bulbous nose, her round face sporting a short dark haircut, and a light brown dress draped around her squat frame. At first impression, she evinced a similar presence to Nº 185's Elvira Nikolaevna.

And unlike Elvira's small, informal cabinet, Rima Alexandrovna's mimicked the ones at the Education Board and factory executive offices. At the front of her desk, a long mahogany table surrounded by six red-cushioned, straight-backed chairs extended into the room. On it were scattered papers, two gray telephones, and a six-inch-high bust of Lenin. A large portrait of the man-god hovered over the soft-backed chair behind her desk. Two bookshelves with trophies and banners stood against the wall opposite tall, Soviet-red-curtained windows.

Rima Alexandrovna appeared relaxed as she asked Valentina to pour three cups of Brazilian instant coffee. Rima Alexandrovna spoke little English, despite being head of a special English-language school. We had a brief conversation before Valentina suggested—in her impeccable English—that we adjourn to her second-floor cabinet.

She led me up a dark stairway into the primary hall. Again, a larger-than-life-sized bronze figure of Lenin on a high pedestal dominated the space, even more grandiloquent than the Lenin downstairs. She took me into the orderly staff room—School N° 185 did not have one—and pointed to where the Class Registers were kept and to the bulletin board, which had instructions for evacuating the school and city in case of nuclear war. We stepped into her crowded cabinet behind the staff room, which she shared with her associate vice-principal in charge of other academic subjects. After pouring each of us another Brazilian instant coffee, she broached the plans she had for me.

"I have devised this schedule for you," she began in her self-assured voice, which I'd first heard when she greeted me at Moskovsky Station. She handed me a schedule typed in Russian on flimsy tracing paper, in triplicate; I struggled to decipher the Cyrillic. As challenging it was for me to speak the language, reading it was more difficult. Why isn't it in English? I wondered, given that I'm an exchange teacher from America?

After some minutes attempting to read it, I asked, "Where is my name?"

"You are *starjour.* It means probationary [no contract] teacher," she said, and added in the same breath, "we have arranged *everything* for you. I hope you will find it to your satisfaction. We would like you to observe some classes first. As you can see from the schedule, you will come on Monday for the third lesson. Meet me here a few minutes before, and I shall take you around."

"May I drop in to visit the school earlier?"

"No that will not be necessary, because then I shall be busy with my students."

I was feeling empty, empty of my American self who wanted to engage, who wanted to commingle with Russians as their colleague. I sensed Valentina intended to plunk me into the middle of a pasture, a lonely cow, away from the hubbub of school life. I could only be a trespasser invited in for brief sojourns, and then returned to the pasture as soon as possible.

With nothing more to say—her perfunctory welcoming done— Valentina stood and indicated it was time for me to leave. As we walked past the impressive Lenin statue and headed downstairs and past the other Lenin icon, I was already missing Irina Nikolaevna's curiosity and Elvira Nikolaevna's energetic welcome. No *Picture of Dorian Gray* under my arm. No invitation to teach a lesson the following Monday; I'm to arrive to observe the third lesson. I am *starjour*. I see myself becoming an interloper, invisible, smothered beneath the cloak of the Soviet red veil, relegated to the surface of the Russian *matryoshka* with few if any opportunities to probe. No conversations in the Russian-speaking Rima Alexandrovna's cabinet, and most likely only formal exchanges with the taciturn Valentina Valentinovna.

I walked two blocks to Nevsky Prospekt and took the N° 26 bus for the twenty-minute ride to 33 Ulitza Voinova—to reconnect with my friends at School N° 185.

TRUE TO HER schedule, Valentina had me observe for the first two days and then teach four lessons a day except Wednesdays. She assigned a specific period for lunch. During each second morning break, she insisted that I join her for a cup of Brazilian instant coffee in her cabinet. She made no arrangements for me to meet with the English Department, nor did she encourage her teachers to mingle with the American.

I ate lunch alone in the canteen, occasionally with another teacher or student. Toward the end of my first month, I spotted four English teachers including one whose class I'd taught that morning. I bought my lunch of watery beet soup, dry bulgur, mixed salad, lukewarm compote, and stale brown bread, and sat down to join them. A chance to connect. Everyone looked up and continued their conversation about family and friends—in Russian.

In the staff room, everyone seemed preoccupied. Hardly anyone took time to talk with me; I expected questions about my life, my teaching, and the United States, especially about education. I hoped they would ask me about my impressions of their school. If I came every day, perhaps the barrier between us might break down. However, I think I spent more time in the bathroom speaking into my cassette recorder.

As the weeks passed, my lessons were restrained, less creative, and conformed more to the norm. Coffees with Valentina did not lead to the insights or revelations I experienced with Irina Nikolaevna. Because of these constraints, I became cognizant of teaching under the yoke of conforming to the Soviet way. It was a dark side of the collective, a part of the *matryoshka* that I'd not seen. Had I been on staff, I would have had trouble committing to the school; I also imagined that I would not have been able to find a way out.

An inspector from the Education Board would have perceived School N⁰ 169 as exemplary, fulfilling Moscow's plans for a proper Soviet education. Following protocol was the school's modus operandi. In addition to Lenin's ubiquitous presence, every room had clear signage, and doors were locked unless a teacher was present. Before school, the inspector would observe monitors taking their roles seriously, recording names of children who had forgotten their indoor shoes. Throughout the day, he would observe cleaning women dutifully sweeping and mopping floors.

He would approve of the teachers' designated cloakroom having its special key kept in a glass-door cabinet in the secretary's office. He'd watch teachers entering daily grades in their Class Record Books and noting disciplinary incidences. During break times, teachers and students on duty wore red armbands on their left arms. Students on classroom duty straightened chairs after each lesson, and at the end of the day, the inspector would observe them mopping floors and washing blackboards.

SCHOOL N° 185's exemplary reputation happened because of Elvira Nikolaevna. Parents, students, and teachers knew she was in charge, her words held sway, and she provided needed resources. She honored Soviet formalities, such as proper assemblies with war veterans; accorded strict adherence to examination rules and expectations; and implemented the required curriculum. At the same time, she allowed her staff freedom; despite her reservations with Gorbachev, she seemed to tolerate his loosening of society's bonds through *perestroika* and *glasnost*. Had Raisa Vladimirovna, my opinionated teacher friend, been a teacher at School N° 169, she would not have survived.

The school had developed a cult of marks. When the 9A-form teachers noticed an increasing number of students skipping lessons, they issued a surprise mid-term report card with as many low grades as possible. "We need to impress upon these hooligans that school is serious business," one teacher told me.

The students laughed it off, knowing they would not face exams until the next year. "Robotman," a quick-witted rebel among his classmates, received all twos. He turned his report upside down.

"Hey, look everyone, I got all fives!"

The mock grading was another example of Soviet *pokazukha*. While teachers knew that these report cards were bogus, they were fulfilling what was expected of them, "pretending to teach while their students were pretending to learn." It was derived from the Soviet adage I heard from a student at School N° 185: "Workers pretend to work, and the State pretends to pay them."

How was it that in one of the most Communist-controlled countries, young people blatantly confronted its feigned authority? They'd been brought up in a strictly controlled collective, watched testimonials on *Vremya*'s nightly news, had years of lessons extolling Soviet achievements, and been indoctrinated in the pageantry of the Great October Revolution of 1917 and the victory over the Nazis in the Great Patriotic War. Yet these students had no hesitation to diss their teachers' effort to control their behavior. Had *pokazukha* become a part of their genes?

IN THE ASSEMBLY hall near the end of my stay on the anniversary of the Great October Socialist Revolution of 1917, Rima Alexandrovna stepped slowly to the podium to open the celebration. Addressing the whole school in her strident, haughty voice, she lauded the half-dozen teachers who were members of the Communist Party (CPSU), introduced the former director of the school, and welcomed the district's Secretary of the CPSU. She turned to Lukásha, the charming, confident, tenth-form leader of the *Komsomol*, the young Communist organization, to ask her to award certificates for her classmates' work at the Camp for Labor and Rest.

You could have heard a pin drop. The room felt charged with formality. Rima Alexandrovna was in charge. I had never seen her in the halls, nor in a classroom. But here she acted in complete control, as if Lenin were looking over her shoulder.

She returned to the podium to hand out certificates to five teachers for their excellence in serving the school. She introduced a group of senior girls, who under the direction of the school's Pioneer Leader, delivered a moving choral rendition celebrating the heroics of youth brigades in the twenties and thirties. The assembly was a model of Soviet decorum. Sitting with teachers near the front of the hall, I felt apart from the proceedings, as if spying on a ritual for Russians alone. But I was there, the exchange teacher, the *starjour*—an obligation no doubt.

After a sustained applause for the choral rendering, Rima Alexandrovna introduced the guest of honor, a veteran in his mid-eighties, who had, as a young boy, witnessed the Great October Socialist Revolution of 1917. In unhurried Russian—Valentina translated for me—Rima Alexandrovna said, "We are honored to have with us a living example of the birth of our great republic. Everyone, please give him a warm welcome."

He stood slowly, and in his dark suit, his lapels suffused with more than two dozen medals, he shuffled to the podium. As he began to speak, his voice hesitated, his Slavic-square, wrinkled face reflecting the weariness of his long life. His words came slowly. Students and teachers began to buzz among themselves. On the stage behind him, Rima Alexandrovna leaned to her right and began to chortle with her assistant, Tatyana. The hall soon swelled into a cacophony, as though the veteran were not there. And, for fifteen minutes! When he finished his inaudible speech, the applause crescendoed—the loudest of the day.

The room had become a free-for-all for teachers, students—and for Rima Alexandrovna. I felt sorry for the veteran. I couldn't imagine what he was thinking. What had begun as a formal ceremony in honor of a momentous historical event had no heart. I felt a deep emptiness. The director's adherence to formal Soviet decorum dissolved to reveal the school's *pokazukha*, a hollow respect for the old man—for the Revolution itself. Before dismissing the assembly, she presented him with a red carnation. Students burst out of their chairs. Rima Alexandrovna gathered the staff for a photograph. She placed the veteran and guests in front, put herself in the center of the middle row, her assistants on either side, and placed the *starjour* directly behind her at the top. At the top, an observer, not a member of the collective.

I CONVINCED VALENTINA to allow me to observe the 9A form for a day. The morning lessons proved routine as expected. Before lunch we came to physics with Ludmilla Andreiyevna, nicknamed "Molecule." From the first moment, the room became boisterous. No one paid attention to her arrival from an adjacent room. Short, bespectacled, and nervous, in a brown shirtdress with an open green cardigan, her hair in a tight bun, she darted about setting up her lecture on the Soviet Union's oil resources. Whenever she looked up, she would shout at a misbehaving student but with no follow-up. I felt her frustration.

She began her lecture. Not five minutes had passed when she called out to Igor, more mature than most in the room, and gave him a two for poor posture. A few minutes later, it was Helen, quiet, gentle, one of the best behaved, scolded for not raising her hand before speaking. Meanwhile, other students were ignoring her and chatting among themselves. I was surprised that she paid no attention to defiant Alyosha's deliberate, loud, metronomic coughing; halfway through the period she'd had enough and dismissed him. Kiril, tall, quiet, sitting in front of me, whispered that Alyosha had wanted to leave class for an early lunch.

Ludmilla asked Dima, short with large dark eyebrows and a budding mustache, to put his homework on the board while she lectured on the workings of the internal combustion engine. Behind Ludmilla's back, Dima pinched information from girls in the front row. Ludmilla asked others to present their homework. André, the last to report, earned a five aided by Katya's prompting. Kiril whispered that André, who was tall, blond, and self-assured, copied homework from girls in the 9B form, who were enamored with his good looks.

Near the end of the lesson, Ludmilla assigned a three-problem quiz. As she was moving equipment from the class to the adjacent lab, students held up papers with answers for other classmates to see. Some shouted information across the aisles. Lukásha, the class

Komsomol leader sitting two seats in front of me, turned around to Kiril for answers; he read from the text on his lap under his desk, although he had told me he knew the answers. By the time the bell rang, the room was in complete bedlam. Students dropped their quizzes into a tray as they dashed out.

Ludmilla Andreiyevna may have been a good teacher earlier in her career, but she no longer seemed to care. She might have been thinking about receiving her pension. Most likely, she did not receive support from administration, as I never saw Rima Alexandrovna in the corridors or classrooms, nor had I seen Valentina or her counterparts for the other academic subjects observing teachers. Ludmilla Andreiyevna was alone in her room, the lonely Molecule, lost from her place in the collective, separated from her colleagues, an addendum to the school day.

Observing her classroom let me in on a failure of the collective. Unless it was guided by a strong leader, it could fall apart. Students in her physics class were forming their own counter-collective. All were engaged in the misbehavior, and no one took the initiative to stop it. I thought about Gorbachev's *glasnost*. He was inviting citizens to take their own positions on matters, positions that might find conflict, a challenging mindset for a culture forged by conformity. I sensed he imagined his people would choose to work toward the good, toward improving society for everyone.

IN MY LAST week, I observed Valentina Valentinovna's 9A English class the day after I'd been their teacher. Sitting in the back, I watched her standing at her desk waiting for students to enter. I can still see her and the class:

> *"Good afternoon." After everyone was seated (not a sound), she said, "I've brought the evidence I promised yesterday when Mr. Thoms was teaching. It's in response to Natasha's claim*

that seven soldiers were killed at the Winter Palace. I'll ask Elena to read the correct evidence at the end of class."

"I now want to hear your reports from the latest news from Vremya.*" Each student spoke, offering "truths," Soviet truths. No controversies. No arguments. All the news from the same source. Simple, clear, true.*

"Today I want to focus on John Reed, the American political writer," Valentina said. (The Soviet curriculum taught children to respect this rebel American.) She then invited each student to give an oral report; she slipped a paper to each of them with a mark, noting mistakes. Near the end of the period, Valentina turned to Elena, who stood, self-assured, studious, and obedient.

"Have you found out about the attack on the Winter Palace, Elena?"

"Yes, Valentina Valentinovna. It says here in Pravda *that only six men were killed. Not seven, as Natasha said yesterday."*

Pravda, *the official newspaper of the Communist Party, meant truth. End of conversation. The bell rang. Valentina dismissed the class.*

Her lesson had fulfilled the dictates of the State. Perfectly. Fully in charge, insisting on good behavior, exerting a quiet formality, inculcating Soviet authority. Her curriculum came from above, and she bequeathed it to her students. What *Vremya* claimed, *Pravda* printed, and textbooks stated was gospel. Besides, the curriculum was too full to concede time for debate and discussion. Her class appeared as an exemplary collective, flawless.

For a moment, I envied Valentina's quiet control, her complete command of the material, her confidence; she probably left school each day without doubts. But I had continuous doubts about my teaching—and believe the doubts have served me well. They stemmed from thinking I should always be doing more: coming better prepared to my lessons, knowing my students and their families better, having more knowledge about my subject, understanding better school politics, and being more conscious of my effect on students and colleagues. These doubts have kept me open to myself, to who I am as a person and as a teacher. Self-awareness when honest has helped me become the teacher I wanted to be.

THE STUDENTS WHO had behaved so well in Valentina's class were some of the same ones who had demonstrated outlandish behavior in Ludmilla Andreiyevna's physics class. Had Valentina's lesson been *pokazukha* designed specifically for the American? I quickly dismissed that idea. She knew the system, the rules, the formality—not only in her classes but for taking care of her *starjour*. She had earned her position as English Department head, because she implemented Soviet practices with expertise. Her students complied, but beneath the radar lurked a Tom-Sawyer-inspired defiance in many of them.

I'd seen some of these same students misbehaving in the corridors and stairwells and listened to their anger in private conversations. *Glasnost* and *perestroika* were unleashing pent-up frustrations. Beneath the *pokazukha* of School N° 169, some students appeared to resent teachers, much more so than I'd observed at School N° 185. Yet, as I saw in Valentina's lesson, her students seemed willing to pretend to learn what their teacher was pretending to teach.

The curriculum was tired and empty. It repeated and repeated and repeated. The humdrum of the six-by-nine-inch, flimsy-paper English texts on Lenin, John Reed, Pioneer heroes, The Black Cat, What Is More Useful?, the Great Patriotic War, et cetera, spoke of a heroic socialism unknown to the children of *glasnost*. They were growing up in a changing society, confessing its political and economic sins and shortcomings every day. Most of them knew that the curriculum was tired and empty.

What if Soviet students had been able to meet with their American counterparts? It would likely have freed them to speak their minds, away from the humdrum of their lessons. And had Zoya's Olya been in the room, the Soviets would have had no hesitation! No doubt Americans would have had their Olyas as well. And coming from two distinct cultures, they would naturally have been curious about one another. The less their teachers were involved, the more likely both groups would have opened up to one another. Young people tend to be more optimistic and open to possibilities.

School N° 169 was living the lie of a model special English-language school, one of twenty-six in the city. In the midst of Gorbachev's *perestroika* and *glasnost,* it perpetrated that all was well with Communism. I wondered how many other schools in Leningrad were clinging to the old Soviet order. Given that Moscow continued to dictate curricula, methodologies, and regulations, I imagine that most school directors toed the line.

Again, as I reflected on the facade of School N° 169, its outer public *matryoshka,* it showed me a Soviet Union before Gorbachev with its ubiquitous pressure from central control. Appearances mattered more than substance. And appearances were enough, or at least it seemed that way for Rima Alexandrovna and Valentina Valentinovna.

The school reflected a Soviet Union enforced from the top that instilled fear—or tried to—on its subjects. It was a nation struggling to maintain its Potemkin-village image in the eye of the world. A superpower, yes, but a coherent, strong first-world country it was not. Had I been a Sovietologist and researched widely, I might have better understood the Russian future. Luckily, I would have four more trips to gather impressions.

THE DAY I left School N° 169, I taught two more classes, after which director Rima Alexandrovna offered me the final proverbial cup of Brazilian instant coffee. She presented me a coffee-table book on Alexander Pushkin with an inscription, which she read in halting English.

Dear Frank,

During two months you were working in our collective, you got to know our teachers and our pupils. You discussed a lot of problems with them. You visited some of them at home. I am sure that our teachers and pupils were hospitable to you. Maybe we have a different opinion of some problems, but I think there can't be a precipice between us. I hope that you are our friend, and we shall wait for your letters, and maybe you shall come again to Leningrad.

Happy journey, Frank

Rima Alexandrovna's gesture would have been offered to any exchange teacher. We never had a serious conversation, never exchanged views. I didn't visit teachers in their homes. I'd been the cardboard-cutout American *starjour*, soon to be tossed into the wastebasket. Foreigners had no place in her domain. I imagined she hardly noticed me.

Yet I discovered a lot about her. I observed her Potemkin-village demeanor at the assembly "honoring" the Great Patriotic War of 1917 in which an old veteran was disrespected yet applauded. Students shared with me the *pokazukha* of her strictness. One tenth-form girl confided that though Rima Alexandrovna appeared very strict, she really wasn't. "We only pretend to listen to her." Others told me that she could be cruel, her asperity upbraiding staff and students.

And one former young teacher confided that when Valentina became head of the English Department, she had to leave school. "I had become close friends with Valentina," she told me, "so when she got the appointment, Rima Alexandrovna's distrust of people being close friends with one another forced me to leave."

Something Rima Alexandrovna learned from Stalin?

Rima Alexandrovna was determined for her school to be a successful show school. She wanted it to be seen as exemplary. A teacher explained that when her daughter returned to visit her friends while an American delegation was visiting, Rima Alexandrovna reprimanded her for not wearing proper shoes—exactly what that meant I was uncertain. I left the school with no fanfare, no appeals to return, only quiet goodbyes. Just as well, because had I stayed for the balance of the year, I would have remained as *starjour,* a probationary teacher. I'd become what I feared might happen in a Soviet school, an interloper. I've never wanted to be seen as a nonentity, outside the community in which I worked. And being a foreigner, an American—at least in this school—made it more difficult. I saw how an authoritarian culture can isolate itself and ostracize its people. I'd penetrated an unexpected layer of the *matryoshka.* I was not invited into the family.

POSTSCRIPT:

Much to my surprise, near the end of my time at the school, Ludmilla Mikhailovna, the cantankerous supervisor from the Education Board, invited me to speak at an in-service workshop to over one hundred Leningrad teachers from the city's special English-language schools. After her kind introduction, I began:

> *Have you ever thought of yourselves and your students as puppeteers of the Soviet State? Have you seen yourselves as passengers on Moscow's curriculum train? Will you consider stepping off this train and take time to listen to what your students have to say. You are living in a time of great change*

in your country. What has been gospel is now being trans-
formed. The strictness of Communism before Gorbachev is
receding, as visitors from the West—I am one—are flocking in
to see who you are and where you are headed.

I have been privileged to teach at two of your schools—Nº
185 and Nº 169—and visited several others. I have come to
know your English curriculum and how your schools func-
tion. I've seen eager children wanting to know more about my
country, about the West. I don't pretend to imagine that our
ways are better. But I know that at least some of your young
people are looking to break out of the strictures of your system.
I know that some of you are as well.

I implore you, then, to step off Moscow's curriculum train
and take time to listen to your students. You will be better for
it. Each child is a drop of rain. Cherish each drop, love each
drop. You should not simply listen to the storm.

Perhaps I stepped outside the boundaries of my invitation as an
exchange teacher. I may have appeared arrogant. Ludmilla turned to
me, smiled, and—curt as always—said, "Thank you, Frank." Despite
the attentive audience, I wonder if she or the teachers heard what I'd
said.

VII
LIKE IN A MOUSETRAP

*"You know, you can do whatever you want with people, everywhere.
That's the most tragic thing. You can turn people into a crowd, then
into a herd, and lead them wherever you want. It can happen in any
country—in yours as well unfortunately."*

Raisa Vladimirovna, October '88

In my search behind the red veil in hopes of penetrating the inner
layers of the *matryoshka,* I found a few teachers who let me in.
Raisa Vladimirovna at School Nº 185 was one. Each time we met, she
offered the American her heart and mind. For reasons I will never
know, she took me in. As if I were her kin. As if I were her confidant.
In May 1987, I returned to her room while she was preparing her
eighth form for their exam.

"Raisa Vladimirovna, why does our society focus on buildings and
factories instead of what has happened to our people?" a student asked.

"It's not that we forget, Katya," she said from her desk in front of
a group of desks clustered in a horseshoe. "Sometimes we did forget.
Conditions were so hard that we forgot to survive as a country—conditions of food, water, economic isolation. Nobody helped us restore
the economy. It was destroyed by the war."

Rising from behind her desk, Raisa Vladimirovna paused. "You remember the figures I gave you about the war? About the most active part of the population, those who were eighteen when the war began? Out of the generation who were seventeen, eighteen, nineteen when the war began—out of every one hundred—only three percent survived the war. The youngest! The best! The most active! The strongest were destroyed by the war.

"And I can give all of you one more figure. Not a single pig was left on the whole territory of Byelorussia and the Ukraine! Not a single pig! Not a single cow!" The room became quiet. "The pigs were all were taken to Germany or eaten by the occupants." She paused. "You can't imagine from what zero we began the reconstruction. It wasn't reconstruction, it was more than reconstruction. It was the beginning of the very beginning. You won't need many figures for your exam. These will be sufficient for what you need to know about the Great Patriotic War."

BARELY FIVE FEET TALL, with wavy, short, gray hair and a resolute look in her shirtwaist dress, she resonated authority through her presence, her discourse. Her tone was sharp. She did not mince words or forsake emotions.

Her classroom was tucked away on the bottom floor in a corner behind the back wall of another classroom. It was the first room in which I taught outside Elvira Nikolaevna's palatial room on the second floor. Instead of having her students sit at tables in rows, she pinched her cherubs into a tight semicircle surrounding her desk, which was piled with bulky dictionaries and scattered papers. She invited me to sit beside her at her desk as she cajoled students into conversations that stretched their English—and their minds. Because I'd heard from other teachers that preparing for exams was not open to foreigners, perhaps I witnessed what I should not have.

In her lessons, Raisa often interjected counter-opinions after her students spoke. She asserted her reactions not only to what they said but to the students themselves. When Donya criticized a war veteran for sounding weak while speaking at an assembly, Raisa cut her off.

"Ah, Donya, they fought better than they speak?" Donya nodded hesitantly. Again in a harsh tone, putting her student firmly in her place—and in front of her peers, "It's good that it was this way, Donya. Otherwise this veteran would not be here, if he spoke better than he fought!"

And in that same lesson, she allowed me to take a turn. I began by asking Nadya, who earned fives [As] in all of her classes, "Why do you do so well in school, Nadya?"

Before Nadya could say anything, Raisa interrupted. "How many students in your form now, Nadya?"

"Thirty," several replied.

"Thirty-one," inflected Raisa. "Nadya's mother is the thirty-first student in the class. She comes to school every second day practically. She knows everything and teaches the girl at home. She makes her work, organizes her life. She does everything! She sits on her shoulders and makes her work. And she loves her, though I think too much. She gives all her life to her daughter, undeservedly."

Raisa paused and added in a calmer tone, "Nadya would not be Nadya if it were not for her mother. Nadya's all right. She is very energetic, very dynamic. Somehow she manages to have. . . well, to give all to everything. Time and energy and heart."

Nadya smiled.

I then asked Masha, who expressed concern about her grade in anatomy, "Can you raise your mark in anatomy before the end of the term?"

"Yes, I can, Mr. Thoms."

"She won't!" interjected Raisa Vladimirovna. "She likes the pictures in anatomy. Look at her! Does she look like a girl who gets fives on test papers? Well, yes, she does look it with her specs. It's very misleading, you know. With her you can't tell."

"You know, Frank," she said to me after the lesson, "I love all my students. Yes, I'm hard on them, I want them to think. They are like family to me." I learned later that Raisa was single and took in children who needed help.

RAISA WAS REFLECTING the Soviet collective mindset. As director, Elvira Nikolaevna spoke openly in front of parents about failing students; Raisa and her colleagues did the same with students in front of their peers. In such moments, I would cringe but say nothing. I was inside another culture, a part of their *matryoshka* I was trying to understand.

While I admired some collective principles, I never considered invoking public rebuke as Raisa did that day with Donya, Nadya, and Masha. The one time that I chose to make an incessant gum-chewing student place his already-well-chewed gum on his nose in front of his peers, I felt more shame than anyone. Had Raisa and her colleagues thought of doing this, they would have had no remorse.

Then came my turn to teach her sixth-formers, an active, engaging group with whom she was more gentle. After a quick retelling of "The Black Cat," lesson five in their textbook, I decided to push the envelope, to move them to think beyond the text.

"Are any of you superstitious like Sam, the cook, or the captain in this story?"

"Oh no!" said several students. Olya, a spindly, tall, dark, straight-haired girl with a prominent Roman nose, who had rubbed her hands together with glee when she saw me in her school for the first time, shouted, "We are not superstitious in the Soviet Union! We do not believe such things!"

"Surely, Olya, you must be superstitious about something."

"No I am not!" Her voice rose. I looked at Raisa sitting in the back, who often chimed in, but she said nothing. I grabbed a piece of chalk and asked Olya if she had a favorite sport.

"Yes, swimming. I like to swim."

"Good, Olya." I turned to the board and drew four stick figures, one of them taller than the others, as if ready to start a race. I pointed to the tallest. "Who is this?"

"Olya, it's Olya!"

"Yes, you're right. Now to tell them apart, I will give each a number. Number seven for the first, a four for the next, an eleven for the third, and for Olya"—I paused for effect—"the number thirteen."

"No! No! No!" Shouted Olya. "We do not use that number!" Others nodded in agreement.

"See, you *are* superstitious!" I said smugly. How clever of me, I thought. I've taught her something.

But I did not anticipate her resolute resistance. I was enjoying a Pyrrhic victory, the cleverness mine alone. Raisa remained quiet. Sensing I'd misplayed my hand, my stomach churned. I was provoking a deeply held Soviet superstition. I walked over to her and put my hand on her shoulder to show empathy—and thinking I could assuage my guilt. Instead of being the clever teacher who thought he could help a student discover a truth about herself, I had chosen to be the arrogant foreigner who willingly trespassed on a cherished belief.

I'm grateful to have acted that way only once. At the same time, I might have opened Olya and her classmates' thinking brains, away from the repetitive acceptance of uncontested cultural norms and textbooks. But my place in School Nº 185 was as a guest. For the most part, I behaved well in seeking to know Russians within the bounds of the Soviet world in which I was given permission to venture.

From the moment we met, Raisa had trusted me. She skipped all formalities and began expounding her views on Gorbachev and education. She opened the door for me to understand her students on their terms. She accepted me as a colleague and allowed me inside where few others had been. I worked to keep our trust and the trust of everyone at the school. But I might have blown it that day with Olya. Without trust, especially in a foreign culture, my teaching would have been a one-way street, where children would have dutifully attended my classes and left as if never having been there. That day with tall and spindly Olya, I learned to accede to Russian idiosyncrasies.

RAISA VLADIMIROVNA AND I had our last conversation in October 1988 when I was leading a tour to Leningrad. We spoke outside Elvira Nikolaevna's cabinet. Maria, the secretary, was typing on a Russian Lubava mechanical typewriter. Over the constant *clack-clack, clack-clack* of keys hitting the black rubber roller, Raisa spoke her mind. (I switched on my tape recorder in my pocket.)

"Now when I'm home, Frank, all I feel like doing is watching TV, nothing else. I have never had such crazy ideas about sitting and watching TV. I always liked to listen to music. But to watch TV, it is degradation." Then lowering her voice, she said, "You know, things are really happening in this country. Not in the economy where things stay the same. I think it's impossible to change. But politically, it's interesting to know."

Clack-clack, clack-clack, clack-clack . . . Maria continued to type. She was unaware of our conversation; she didn't understand English.

"I read a lot, but TV is taking up more of my time. I meet people less. I don't go places. It's amazing. I don't like the way I live now, but I can't *stop* it. TV is like a narcotic. For the first time I've not learned from books but from TV! I used to learn things from books—not to learn but somehow to absorb, you know. With TV I just listen and learn. I have somehow fenced myself off from people, from life. You know, I enjoy it this way, and that's what I'm afraid of. It frightens me."

Barely taking a breath, she continued, "Many blank spots in our history are being revealed. Things we didn't know. Of course, I knew more than the average citizen. I just had some ways to know. But I didn't *know* about many things at all. I *suspected* them, but I didn't know. And now we speak about such things, so many things have become known."

"Discovering these blank spots must be fascinating for you, Raisa."

"It's fascinating." She sighed. "But it is *killing*, as well. It's killing, and I mean it. Knowledge hurts." She paused and sighed again. "It's just . . . you don't want to learn any more. Sometimes you don't want to live any more. Our whole history is a tragedy, you know."

"Yes, I've been aware of this for a long time," I said quietly.

"You knew it, Frank, but we *feel* it."

"You've read *Animal Farm*?" I asked.

"Sure, I read it twenty-five years ago when I was in university, but it didn't apply. We never knew we were reading about ourselves. This is the greatest tragedy, that we lived in the middle of all this and managed not to know."

"As if you were in an eye of the storm?"

"More like in a mousetrap, Frank, as if in a mousetrap. You know, I never believed that the German people never knew about the concentration camps. I thought, well, they were lying—and we didn't know about our own!" She hesitated. "You know, you can do whatever you want with people, everywhere. That's the most tragic thing. You can turn people into a crowd, then into a herd, and lead them wherever you want. It can happen in any country—in yours as well, unfortunately.

"People will never see what they don't want to see and will manage to be happy, to raise children, to love. And you know, millions in our country were exterminated, and people still managed to be happy. And in Germany as well. They marched, sang songs, laughed, loved, and were not afraid to give birth to children."

"Why didn't people know, Raisa?"

"Well, when people don't want to know, they don't know. And it is sincere; it is a sincere sense of knowledge. You know, it is like wishful thinking. When you don't want to see, you don't see. When you don't want to know, you don't know . . . . There is something basically wrong with mankind."

"All of us?"

"Not all." She sighed. "There are those people who are different. I think the earth stands on them. They hold the world on their shoulders. And here in Russia, we had some, very few. Maybe only a few, because if their head stuck out, it was cut off. That's all." (Raisa alluded to the conversation with her eighth-formers before exams.) "Now we are rid of *so many* bright heads. The genetic pool was lost, because the *best* were executed. It was not just by random, but the best. It's millions of the best. It is the tragic truth."

Again she paused and came back to herself. "Somehow I am in a bad mood and have been for two years. It makes me irritated."

"Have your kids suffered?"

"They have. They have, because I want too much from them, because I know that it is they who should rectify things, and they are not fit. It is not the generation that can make things better. But, I submit, they are the next generation. And we don't have another one . . . and almost with resignation, maybe they will produce a better one . . . ."

Clack-clack, clack-clack, clack-clack . . .

WHILE I WAS writing this book, I learned that Raisa Vladimirovna had died. It's hard to imagine, her zest seemed that it would last forever. She would have understood the 2016 election in the US. And again, I'm reminded of some of the last words she ever said to me:

You know, you can do whatever you want with people, everywhere. That's the most tragic thing. You can turn people into

a crowd, then into a herd, and lead them wherever you want.
It can happen in any country—in yours as well unfortunately
. . . you know, it is like wishful thinking. When you don't want
to see, you don't see. When you don't want to know, you don't
know.

I wonder what she would have thought about Vladimir Putin's ascendency—and about the rise of Trump in America. My bet, she would have seen Putin coming, would not have approved, and would have continued to be herself. Meeting her in the time of Gorbachev was a privilege, an open window for this American into her Soviet world. I imagine she would have done the same for me today.

VIII
LOOK THROUGH THE FINGERS

She reached into her book bag and handed me a transparent Bic ballpoint pen with a slip of paper having tiny black lettering, the formulas required for the test, wrapped around the ink reservoir.

She, October '86

She sat with her athletic friend at a front table pushed against my desk. Relaxed, her head tilted, unwilling to sit erect or raise her right hand at the elbow, she leaned her fifteen-year-old self in a slight slouch. I remember the concentration in her small eyes as she listened. Her smile, frequent but never complete. At the break, she abruptly stepped in between a teacher and me to take me to see the gymnasium. It was my first day in her school.

In my third week, she invited me to visit her communal flat not far from school. No one—teachers or the director—had invited me to their homes. I had been used to spending time in the homes of families, one of the joys of being a teacher. Her parents welcomed me into their one-room flat and shared kitchen and bathroom. In addition to the standard Soviet furniture and accouterments, which I'd seen in Natasha's flat, it had two televisions and a VCR, which played black-and-white music videos.

We had a delightful dinner and conversation; she translated for her parents and me.

Her parents were bright, engaged, and beginning to grasp the potential of Gorbachev's path. Her mother, attractive, dark-haired with a broad, infectious smile, worked at a produce shop. She was satisfied with simple pleasures and tolerated her husband's indulgences. She was an excellent cook.

Her father wanted more. In conversation his eyes lit up, his hands gestured supporting his words, his Russian becoming more rapid when making a point. He was a good match for his wife. Vivacious, gregarious, and often wearing a big grin, he worked at a production plant and was frustrated with the lack of incentives to reward his efforts. He put energy into projects outside the workplace; he secured tickets to performances and art exhibits and conducted tours to Poland and Czechoslovakia. He preferred private *banyas* and cultivated friendships with artists. One evening, when driving me back to my hotel, he proposed, in his broken English, that I find him an attractive university student who could teach him English. He may have had more on his mind. I wasn't surprised. It was as if he were looking out the window for something not there.

She loved both her parents but was closer to her father. "He seems to understand the real me," she told me as we walked in Tavrichesky Park. "He knows what I am thinking, knows what I want. I like his willingness to find ways to join the new economy."

Several weeks after being in her flat, I learned that her invitation had cost her—because the director's policy had been that communal flats were off limits to foreigners. Despite her superior facility in English, the director denied her participation in a TV space-bridge with Seattle. Her best friend told me that, at a class meeting, the director reprimanded her in front of her peers for her forward behavior. (I wish I'd been allowed to attend class meetings, but I was not.) And no doubt the director knew that she and I had numerous conversations outside of school. After all, the director's husband was KGB.

She spoke freely about school, the director, her teachers, and her classmates. She criticized without remorse and praised without sarcasm. We conversed on the streets, in her flat, in classrooms, on park benches, at the Café Tarakan, and in metro stations. She was the first to reveal the dark underside of Soviet student life, the common practice of *shparlgaka* (cheating) and the use of *shpora* (crib sheets). One late afternoon in an empty classroom, she and I spoke about her test in chemistry, not her major subject.

"I did well," she said with a smirk, "but it was hard." She reached into her book bag and handed me a transparent Bic ballpoint pen with a slip of paper having tiny black lettering—the formulas required for the test wrapped around the ink reservoir. "It took me a long time to prepare this and fit it inside," she said, "but it was worth it!" She received a four out of five on the chemistry test, a respectable mark; I still have the pen.

Chemistry was not her strength. Because she and her classmates had to earn respectable grades in all subjects, including those outside their specialties, making *shpora* thrived. The night before her chemistry final, she prepared index cards with answers for the twenty-five exam questions. In the exam room, she selected a card from the tray and returned to her seat; she matched it to the answer in her pocket. When her turn came, she presented her answer to the panel, which included the director, the vice director, and her teacher. After the exam, she left the room and shared her cards with her classmates. Such chutzpah, I thought.

"Did the teachers know you had ready-made cards in your pocket?"

"Sure, they did. They knew. The director knew for sure but looked the other way." She demonstrated turning her head sideways and putting her hand with spread fingers next to her eye. "It's called, *smotret skvoz palcy*—to look through the fingers, that is, 'not see.'"

"Could they check your pockets?"

"We're not accustomed to having them checked. It's impossible."

"But could they if they wanted to?"

"Yes, of course, they could check."

"So they are on your side, aren't they?"

She pauses. "Yes, but it's not for us. It's for them."

"So you and your classmates have understood this for a long time?"

"Yes, everybody knows. Everybody knows. By the way, Frank, I didn't cheat at English, literature, or composition exams. They're important courses for my university, so I had to do well. When it comes to getting into university, cheating has no place. If I had cheated, it would have shown up later—bad for me, bad for the school."

She received a four for physics using the same process. *Shpora* was a positive catch-22 for everyone, or so it seemed. Teachers expressed pleasure when their students scored well, especially when earning a place at university. The more successful their students, the better they felt, the more recognition they received from their superiors. She received the necessary grades for university, the school earned credit for the success of one of its own—and the Soviet educational authorities were circumvented once again. It was *pokazukha,* and everyone knew it.

The more she divulged about cheating on tests and exams, the more I understood how she and her classmates needed to manipulate the system. Teachers were required to enter a grade into the form's Class Record Book for each student after every class. She and her classmates would appeal to teachers to change their grade—all centering on their wish to get into university. She shared some examples.

"Sometimes, Frank, there are special competitions to get into programs at an institute. If you don't have any threes [considered a poor grade], you need only to pass one exam instead of three. I understand, for example, that my English teacher will never give me a three. If I have a bad day, she will let it pass. I think this is fair. She is a good teacher.

"If, for example, a teacher gives you a three, it means you have not done well. It is necessary then to come to the teacher and speak with her. Whenever I did, I would explain that this subject was not necessary for me. A low grade would prevent me from doing well over all. For example, in PT [physical training] I asked the teacher to give me a four in spite of him having given me a three, because I had to have a four. Nothing was said as to why. He just did it."

And she had a rebellious streak.

"In the fourth form when our teacher was ill, we had lessons with a different teacher. Every English lesson, he consulted the dictionary. It was strange, as we thought that a teacher should know everything—and he didn't."

Later, she told me about the Moscow play *Dear Elena Sergeyevna*.

"It's about three kids who left their math exams blank so they could write them after the exam and get a better mark. These kids went to their teacher with their blank exams and told her why they needed excellent marks.

"Well, these kids forced the teacher, Elena Sergeyevna, to give them her key to the box with the exams and answers. She died after that I think, I don't remember. I think all teachers should see this play. They could learn, for instance, that ours is a bad system that requires kids to have excellent marks in math and science when they are applying to the philological faculty at the university."

She never failed to reflect honestly. In sharing her inner thoughts, she was letting me into her inner self, as if I were her lifelong Russian friend. She was unaffected by the red veil that seemed to surround others in her class. Her first act—abruptly interrupting the teacher who was talking to me on my first day in her school—spoke volumes about her maverick persona, about doing things her way.

SHE WAS AMONG the brightest in her class. In the fourth form she was Pioneer Leader and wore the coveted "Land of October" pin. Through the sixth form, she was a model Soviet youth, earning high marks and the respect of her teachers. Despite her understanding of the pretentiousness of Soviet expectations upon children and teachers alike, she was glad to have been Pioneer Leader. "I got to go to a special Pioneer camp during the summer," she told me with a smile. "It was a wonderful experience."

In the spring of her eighth-form year—the year I met her—her school had purportedly become "overcrowded." The director, having dismissed weaker students from the school, threatened to reshuffle the eighth forms to make them more balanced unless two students volunteered to move. She and her athletic friend volunteered. They were willing to leave a "family" that had been together for eight years—much to the deep chagrin of their classmates, some of whom cried.

The communal mindset resided deep in Soviet Russian life. I thought about its origins during the reigns of the early tsars. To survive oppression under autocratic rule and life in a challenging climate, Russians have stayed close for generations. And bearing the loss of millions of lives during Stalin and World War II, and the failure of the promise to build Communism under the Bolsheviks and—reminded by the enforced scarcities of daily life—solidified the perseverance to dwell close to one another. A trait deep in the Russian soul.

WHEN I RETURNED the next year to her city to teach in a different school, I kept in touch with her. I would usually find her at her school. We'd take walks or go to a café, sometimes just us, other times with her friends. In one of our encounters—I remember it well—I expressed my frustration with the formality of my new school, much more rigid than hers.

"I can't believe these students all speak about America with one voice: 'The US is propagating the arms race, inflicting capitalistic oppression, invoking imperial aggression, creating massive unemployment, and putting countless homeless in the streets!' No matter what age, they all say the same things! That's so frustrating!"

She looked at me, dropped her eyes, and looked up. "There's a difference between what we want to say and what we need to say."

She had spoken like this before, about how *pokazukha* underlay Soviet life; it went to great length to shield society's realities. I've noticed, too, that American schools at the local level tended to set up similar shields to hide what was not working—their own *pokazukha*. Parents' night, for example, often became a front for success, hiding the idiosyncrasies that pervaded everyday school life. We might not be as far apart from one another as we think, I thought.

I saw an example of feigned concern at her school when I returned the following spring. Teachers were in a tizzy about the upcoming exams. One of my favorite teachers, shaking in her gnomish body with her short, tightly curled hair and round, thick spectacles, ran up to me.

"Oh, my gosh, Frank! We will not have the exam questions in advance! Instead, they will be delivered the morning of the exam. We do not know what topics the board will choose. And they will be judged by outside examiners. This has never happened! We are caught in a bind. I am worried! I am worried!"

The issue proved bogus. Regardless of the topics the board selected, there would be no outside examiners. The director and teachers would decide the results; they always had. And once the first group took exams, everyone would know the topics. In the end, no one was surprised; the questions were nearly the same. It was a self-imposed charade—another *pokazukha*—with everyone saying what they needed to say. Was it for my benefit? (I doubt it.)

ONE YEAR AFTER she took me to her parents' communal flat, her father had arranged at considerable cost to move into a three-room apartment where she would have her own room.

"My parents are proud. They want a comfortable flat where they can entertain friends, but it is very expensive. I am worried. I help in any way I can. I earned money on a collective farm last summer, which I gave to my father to buy furniture. Now, we want to buy a telephone, which is expensive, as we are not in the city center any-more. It takes me an hour on the bus to get to school."

Still, she was eager to show me her new home. Since it was not a communal flat (and far from the school) she had no hesitation to invite me. And this time, because I was not under the jurisdiction of her director, she would not be reprimanded.

I arrived as planned at four-thirty at Moskovskaya metro station. She asked me to ride in the last wagon, close to where she would be waiting. Stepping off the train, I did not see her; I sat and waited on a nearby bench. After everyone had left, I looked up and spied her across the way in jeans, legs crossed, wearing a long deep blue coat nearly touching the ground. Was this the same girl who, in her blue synthetic school uniform, looked so much younger, more like thir-teen or fourteen? Perhaps it was the uniform. I was used to teaching in front of a fashion show of college-town eighth-graders competing for attention. Sitting on that bench, she would have fit right in.

We left the station to board a bus. We arrived at her building, went upstairs, and greeted her parents. Before dinner she showed me her room. (In the communal flat, she had slept on a pull-out couch in the one room.) She pointed to her three stuffed dolls placed on a red-and-black bedspread against the wall, five more on top of a bookcase with shelves that had collections of miniature dolls, small cars, jungle animals, and books. A two-foot-tall plastic balloon figure stood in the corner. A giant photograph of Michael Jackson covered the wall behind her desk. I had trouble matching the decor with the grown-up girl sitting before me.

Her desk was neat, a couple of school texts and bluebook-sized notebooks set in the middle. Atop her clothes cabinet was an unplugged television, which her father had purchased with money that she earned in a shop over the summer. We talked for nearly a half hour as she rubbed the worry stone I'd given her when I'd last seen her the year before. I heard her reaching beyond her room's furnishings. Her tone of voice was calmer, deeper, and quietly firm. Close to seventeen years old, her schoolgirl mannerisms seemed to have retreated, and her newfound maturity showed in her choice of words.

Her mother called us to dinner. Delicious food and drink, vodka and cognac surrounded the conversation and laughter. She engaged as an adult; she translated enough to let me in on the conversation, allowing me to feel part of her family. From the day we met, my role in our relationship had been more the recipient than the giver. She saw me as a doorway into the Western world; I became more and more the listener, the receptor of her thoughts, ideas, and wisdom. More often than not, she would challenge me. I was grateful for the teacher in me to take a back seat.

In a touching moment, she presented her father's best friend with a miniature doll she'd bought in Poland, a gift he received in tears. And, late in the evening, she danced with her father—their movement a symbiosis.

WE MET FOR the last time in October 1988, when I was leading a tour. Now in university, she came to my hotel along with some of her classmates, who were also in institutes or university. We snuck by the doorman to my room (Soviets were not allowed in international hotels). In a spirited conversation, her friends revealed that they never wanted to visit their teachers. I was surprised at their enmity. When teaching in their school, I had warm images of their relationships.

She, ensconced on a bed quietly listening, spoke up.

"Teachers tell us what is necessary. They have two faces, one as a human being, one as a teacher. Without their masks, they could not be teachers."

The others looked at each other and nodded in agreement.

As I absorbed her words, I thought back to the times her director may have been wearing a mask and was being not honest with me— again a *pokazukha*. I recalled the teachers who had spoken harshly about me after I left. And I wondered about my own mask. And about the masks of my colleagues.

SHE WROTE LETTERS often. In nearly all of them, she went into great detail about boyfriends, lots of different ones. Sometimes she'd write paragraphs about the ebb and flow of each one.

In an early letter, she expressed frustration with her Greek major at university—she really wanted to study English. She often waxed philosophical with thoughts beyond her years.

> *Hello dear teacher,*
>
> *I would like to know your literature, your people, and everything about your country. I understand, however, I must learn Greek, because the more languages I know, the more chances I will have for future work. So here are two forces, which a man has inside struggling always: what you want to do and what you must do, what you love and what you need. And because of that, great disappointments.*

After detailing her frustration with three boyfriends—in vivid detail—she concluded the letter.

You know, today I tried to understand why it's you to whom we all write things and tell you things which we have so deep inside. How do you use our thoughts? Are they necessary and interesting for you? Is it difficult to hear parts of our souls? Do you discuss about us with people you know? Or maybe we are just a curiosity? How would I feel if I received such letters? Are you doing it as a teacher, a man, or as a human being? I'd like to know it.

Please write me only what you really think about. I wouldn't like you to be my new disappointment.

Her letters seemed to free her soul. I had been under deeper scrutiny than I imagined when with her. But when I wrote, I spoke from my heart. I could not imagine writing any other way. For me to listen to her spilling her thoughts and not do the same would have violated our friendship.

And her questions pressed me to ponder how forthright I'd been as a teacher. Was I willing to take independent stands despite pressures from those in authority? Was I able to stand for what I believed in the face of criticism? Would I be honest in the face of adversity?

In two letters, she expressed her paradoxical relationship with her school.

Hello dear teacher,

I hate my school. I understand that it is not nice to write such things about the place where I spent ten years of my life, but it's the truth. I simply can't find anything good that school gave me . . . . Yes, it taught me how to live and opened my eyes for some things, but that was all . . . . I think the teacher must understand me, my mood, or at least try to do it. Years ago, I think they did. But now our teachers have their concerns with their husbands and children.

And now I think that if I cry at our Last Bell, it will be only because of the fact that the childhood is over and nothing more.

And in a later letter about school:

Hello dear teacher,
    I don't know exactly what school gave me. From the point of view that school was a special time, it gave my first friend who is now in your country but still remembers me; it gave me my first boyfriend who is now married; it gave me the first boyfriend with whom I first understood love (or began to) but who now has another girl. In school, I understood that people are different, and that I ought not to believe people but still do. And of course, school gave me many lessons in communication. That's all.

I was surprised at her expressing her lack of respect for her school—and then I wasn't. She was an independent thinker who never hesitated to offer her point of view. Underneath her distaste for her teachers, she expressed empathy but nevertheless admonished them for their failures. And in her upper form years, she rebelled against the school's restrictive expectations, expectations foisted upon all Soviet students. She knew what she wanted, what she could get. Stepping away from the school's tight stricture—an imposition on everyone—she chose to speak her mind, to act without impunity.

One of her most intriguing letters came in June 1989 after her Last Bell. She and fellow graduates took a radical path and chose to honor only the teachers they respected and ignore the rest. Gorbachev's effort to open Soviet society had worked its way down to where students had the courage to break protocol. She'd spearheaded the idea.

That's why our performance was very warm and pleas-
ant. We did everything honestly, not as classes usually did.
We intended to cry at the end, but tears ran from my eyes at
the beginning when the first-graders congratulated us with the
end of school.

Again in her philosophical musings, she went on:

I can't say I feel anything sad in my soul that I'll never
take lessons again. Though we didn't love some of our teach-
ers, they are people with their own features, who are close to
us because we know them for a long period of our life, which
is very important to every person. By their attitude to us, to
our love stories, we can judge them. But everybody knows that
remembering something whole, one thinks only about the
best, forgetting the worst.

And she continued to make frank comments about me. When
she was upset with what I wrote, she would take paragraphs to tell
me. One of her themes was wanting me to be true to myself. One
example:

I would like to wish you always be yourself and never con-
ceal your real feelings and emotions—especially when you are
with your friends. Maybe it is unusual for us Russians, but
friends will always understand you.

And once in the middle of long letter, an unexpected reflection:

About your being romantic . . . I don't see it in having
relationships happening in two faraway places (in all mean-
ings). Just I think you belong to that type of man who can see

something in every woman. It's an art. And even if sometimes
it makes shit, I respect it.

In each of her letters, she was reaching further inside our relationship, as if she wanted nothing to be left unsaid. Her tears at the
Last Bell, her thoughts about remembering teachers, her repeated
desire—her insistence, in fact—for me to be myself. But her venture
about my being romantic took me by surprise. I never imagined
her imagining me as "that type of man," as any type of man. I saw
myself as me, at most as teacher and friend, never thinking that I was
a "type." Perhaps, as the young grow into adulthood, they become
closer to us who are already there. Her openness diverged from other
Russians I'd observed, many of whom tended to hide themselves
behind their personal red veils while all the while eager to find out
who I was.

And her wish for me on my birthday, another plea, again asking
for honesty:

Happy Birthday to you. I wish you not to feel your fifty-one
years and just be what you are and what I know you.

SHE LOVED HER city. She wrote about it on the night that she and her
father drove me to Finland Station to say goodbye for the last time.

When we left you at the station, I asked my father to show me
the city in the night lights. It was beautiful. After driving to
the Petrogradskaya side of the city and through the center, we
drove to the Pulkovo International Airport. I can't describe
how it was. Leningrad is exciting in the evening. I simply have
no words to describe it. Maybe it's not so interesting for you,
but our feelings were as if we were lovers. We came home

at two o'clock. I think I will never forget it, but it's strange.
Nobody understands why I was so happy.

I loved her city too. But not my first foray at the airport, disdaining its darkness, feeling fear before the olive-green-uniformed customs *apparatchik* who could have turned me away. My best memory of her city was the glow of the first of its beloved White Nights in June, the eve of my departure that spring when I came on my own to her school. A city built on a swamp, holding its own magic. She and I shared that.

A YEAR LATER, one of her closest friends wrote me:

> *Hello Frank,*
>
> *I saw her in the beginning of October—she was happy and beautiful. Yes, I've never seen her so nice, lovely, and beautiful. Maybe she is so charming because she is waiting for a baby? Don't know. But they say pregnancy makes women, each woman, more beautiful than she is. I enjoyed talking with her. She's delightful!*
>
> *And you know, Frank, it was a great surprise for me to find that she is married and waiting for a baby. My little friend, I thought, I can imagine you as a wife, but not as a mother, you're so graceful, so small and charming. When I saw her, I felt that she's really a mother (a future mother, that is), a woman who will do everything for her child. But still she's a lovely angel for me.*
>
> *Is it a surprise for you to hear all this?*

Yes, it was—and it wasn't. Her fetish about boys had lured her into pregnancy. Yet it contradicted her deep desire to study languages and use her newfound knowledge. She'd been at the top of her class, recognized for her intelligence. When ostracized by the director, she had held her own and later led her class into doing the Last Bell her way. With her new Swedish husband and baby, her path would shift.

She has lived in Sweden for nearly thirty years, divorced, happy, having been a good mother to her son. Had she stayed in Leningrad—now St. Petersburg—she'd be holding to her opinions, expressing them whenever she could. But motherhood may have domesticated her, enough to stay behind the scenes. If she returned home, I could see her being well situated, perhaps in her parents' flat, as they have moved to Cyprus. She's skilled at the computer, and because of her language proficiencies, a good translator. On Facebook and through occasional emails, she appears happy. I'm grateful that she trusted me enough to speak honestly—and that I paid attention to who she was becoming.

IX
PODSKAZKA, SHPARLGAKA, AND LYING

"Of course we prompt each other," confided my young friend Nikolai from the 8A form . . . . "It is an important part of our schooling. Without it, our class would not be able to get our work done . . . . It is important to help my friends, more important than helping myself!"

Nikolai N., November '86

Podskazka

My first day teaching at School N° 185. The first period. Fifteen-year-olds discussing Oscar Wilde's *The Picture of Dorian Gray.* Receptive, orderly, calm, curious, outspoken. The next four periods became a tsunami. Little ones apprehensive at seeing the American stepped into Elvira Nikolaevna's palatial room to stare at him. Bustling in different directions, they fell into their desks in pairs; fidgeting, they took out paperback texts, pens, paper. Oh, the fidgeting. Their teacher sat in the back. All eyes on the American in his olive-green jacket.

I asked for first names only and noted where they were sitting so I could call on them by name. I asked questions from the text, to discover what they knew. Silence. Another question. And another.

Some cajoling. A boy's right hand shot up, elbow on the desk. I acknowledged him. He stood. Frozen. His eyes looking up. Was he afraid? Did he know the answer? Then I heard the whispers. From classmates. Sometimes, from the teacher. He answered. I nodded. He sat down. I asked another question from the text. The same pattern, again and again and again.

Every time a child hesitated to answer a question—even for a few seconds—the whispers came. The longer the hesitation, the louder the whispers, soon sounding like a cacophony of locusts. If still no answer, the teacher leaned in and whispered, loud enough for me to hear. Meanwhile, I pleaded, "I want to hear from Yuri, please give him time to think about his answer." "Please, please, let Natasha speak, I want her answer, not yours." My appeals fell on fallow ground.

Twenty minutes later, I asked a question away from the text—and all hands went up! Not to answer but to talk to the American, to be recognized. No raised elbows on the desk; some jumping out of their chairs. I was asking questions about them, about their school, their lives.

OF THE PEDAGOGIES practiced in Soviet schools, *podskazka* proved to be the most bewildering. No matter how I counteracted, it persisted. No teacher seemed concerned.

"Of course we prompt each other," confided my young friend Nikolai from the 8A form, one of the most articulate students in his English section and curious about nearly everything. "It is an important part of our schooling. Without it, our class would not be able to get our work done. Teachers give us a mark every day, so we must be ready for every class. But there is too much homework. We have to help each other. It is important to help my friends, more important than helping myself!"

"Oh yes, it is better for me to help others than to excel. To do any less would be awful," said thoughtful, gentle, wide-eyed Tanya, conveying her infectious smile while sitting between Nikolai and me in the Café Tarakan.

I heard the same sentiment in Tallinn, Estonia. After I observed a class, Irina, an ebullient seventh-former, confided to me why it was important for her classmate to know what she knew. "If I don't help her, she gets a bad mark. I *must* help her! She doesn't want a bad mark!"

Three thousand miles east in Alma-Ata, Kazakhstan, Ira, a tenth-former, one of the quietest in his class, told me, "*Podskazka* is a form of friendship."

PROMPTING KINDLED THE collective spirit. It allowed students to keep pace with the heavy demands of the curriculum. No time to waste, no time to pause, no time for reflection. Without prompting, silence, a silence denoting failure. Prompting ensured that everyone "learned," that slower students wouldn't be left behind. Lessons sounded like symphonies, voices overlapping voices. Prompting maintained the collective, kept everyone in line. It replaced personal responsibility. Discouraged personal initiative.

And prompting served as a mouthpiece for perpetuating the system's expectations. The whispers encouraged repeating the same information. Stand up, listen for a word if needed, give an answer, sit down. Again, again, again, again . . . . No chance to discuss, to argue. What "we" know was more important than what "I" know.

I watched a downside of this endemic Russian trait the day I observed quiet, shy, reticent Luba, a recent transfer into the 5A form at School N° 185. She came from a troubled home, her uniform unkempt, her English deficient; she was a poor student in other subjects as well. Anticipating the prompting, I asked her questions that a classmate had just answered. Each time, she jumped to her feet, stood rigid, freezing her face, eyes at two o'clock toward the ceiling (typical when searching one's brain for an answer) and waited for help. It always came.

Prompting enabled her to appear to be keeping up with her classmates. But it denied her the chance to learn, to discover her own abilities. Her teachers had given up on her potential. At the end of the eighth form, she would be destined to be one of the early leavers. Luba was buried inside a collective system that sought not to distinguish but to blend. An aspect of the *matryoshka* that, in the long run, did not serve Russians well.

WHENEVER I VISITED a Soviet school, each class performed its script. I would step into a room, children would stand in unison, and the teacher would invite me to sit in the back. She would begin her performance as producer and director. After each question— requests to retell the text—children would raise their right hands at the elbow. When called upon, a child would stand and recite the answer—if she knew it. Any hesitation invoked *podskazka*. Quiet at first, louder if necessary. The same routine everywhere—well, almost.

During my first trip to Moscow in October 1985, our tour delegation visited School N° 40—a show school. I recalled sitting in the back of Tatyana Popelyanskaya's room and observing her engage students in a dialogue about John Reed's romanticism. Before Gorbachev instituted *glasnost*, she dared to ask them to think. No *podskazka*. Despite students sitting in pairs at tables in rows, her teaching reminded me of my circle discussions with eighth-graders. She probably had been teaching that way for years.

Had Tatyana been placed in a show school to seduce foreigners into thinking that Russian students were being taught to think? Was she a tool of the Soviet State? And did she know it? If she was for real, she was circumventing Soviet pedagogy, which was rote and routine. To have discussions would have been oxymoronic.

I was grateful that I would later observe teaching practice in four other schools—and have opportunities to teach in them. And, much to my delight, I would find other teachers who taught as Tatyana Popelyanskaya did that day in front of me.

Shparlgaka

"I write information on my thighs just above my skirt," said Tatyana from the 10A form gleefully. "I write mine inside my jacket," replied her classmate, Alyosha. "I devised a way to imprint information with a sharp point on my plastic notebook cover that I can read when held at a proper angle to the light," added Misha. "And I like the new ballpoint pens with windows at the top. When I push the button, information appears," said Dima.

Stories about *shparlgaka* abounded. Zoya Anatolyevna of Moscow School Nº 21 corrected Illya's exam in the director's office so he could have a three instead of a two. She told me about another student who managed to copy all the time. "I even asked this student to sit in front of me for a test, but he still managed to copy without me knowing how. Then, I found out that he put a piece of paper on his seat between his legs and read from it!"

A former student from School Nº 169 recounted with glee her favorite *shparlgaka:* "We got really tired of writing cribs for all the exam questions, Mr. Frank. Instead, we each wrote answers to only four or five of them. Then we hid them in the exam room under rags, piles of papers, wherever we could find a place. It was so great! The teachers paid no attention. When we were writing the exam, they would leave the room, lock the door, and have tea." And her last remark, "It would have been a sin if we *didn't* cheat!" *Shparlgaka* was embedded so deeply in the culture—indeed, as a meme—that I doubt she could have envisaged another way to succeed in exams.

Shparlgaka was not new to the Gorbachev era. A former teacher told me that thirty years before, she knew of a physics student who helped a less able friend. After this student, whose name came earlier in the alphabet, took his exam, he made a faint red mark in a corner on the back of the card that he had selected. When his friend's turn came, he found that card among the twenty-five in the tray. Having the answer from his friend, he fared well, "earning" a four.

Shparlgaka, like *podskazka,* served the collective. Unlike the United States, where students would cheat to get ahead, Soviet students cheated to help one another, the better ones helping the weaker. My young friend Nikolai from School N° 185 referred to *shparlgaka* as *bolshaya naglost,* "big insolence, impudence or effrontery" or figuratively, "the teacher is near but not looking." As with prompting, cheating enabled more students to succeed.

My good friend, Misha Baushev, one of my best sources about all things in Soviet schools, wrote in a letter:

> *I was in the US visiting a class of a professor friend. He asked the Americans and the Russian immigrants in the room: "Would you help a friend during an exam?" One hundred percent of the Americans said "no" and one hundred percent of the Russians said "yes."*

"Teachers *know* that students come to exams with *shpora,*" Zoya Anatolyevna asserted. "Cheating is not a problem if the teacher looks the other way [*smotret skvoz palcy*]. She knows, but as long as she doesn't see, it does not become a problem. Besides, in preparing their *shpora,* they are learning." (I recalled "she," who prepared with great effort a slip of paper with chemistry formulas inserted into her transparent Bic ballpoint pen.)

Prompting and cheating provided knowledge for students who needed it. Without them, the system would have ground to a halt. Imagine a society built on a hollow educational system, one that purported to be rigorous, demanding, and coveting excellence, only to model Grigory Potemkin's false villages. A massive *pokazukha* foisted on the world—and more insidious, on its own people.

Cheating works in all societies for different reasons for different people. In schools or universities in the US, some students cheat for as long as they can get away with it. Athletes cheat using performance-enhancing drugs. Politicians cheat and invoke denial after denial and keep on cheating. And older people cheat themselves when reconstructing their bodies to look younger. In the Soviet Union, the role of *shparlgaka* was embedded deep inside the culture, necessary to its survival, necessary for the society to be able to justify itself.

IN OCTOBER 1988, in my conversation with the feisty, sharp, sardonic, yet gentle English-language teacher, Kristi Tarand at Estonia School Nᵘ 7, she expressed her deep understanding of how the Soviet Union's mutually dependent-based system set back hope for the future.

"There is a very bad need for learning, and now when an organ of man is not used to it, it atrophies," she said wearily. "This has happened to the brain. When everybody says what you must do next, your brain doesn't work when suddenly you have to decide for yourself. We are so used to doing things we are told, Frank. We need to start putting our brains to work. But it is very hard for teachers, not because we are afraid or pessimistic, but because we do not have enough information, not enough knowledge. We don't know. We don't know."

Kristi was reflecting the consequences of a system that was not only authoritarian but pretended, supported by *podskazka* and *shparlgaka*. I connected best with those teachers who did not pretend, like Tatyana Popelyanskaya, Raisa Vladimirovna, Zoya Anatolyevna, Irina Nikolaevna, and Kristi Tarand. They were willing to probe beneath the Soviet red veil by asking their students to think—and by sharing their insights with me.

Kristi's words portended the return of State television under

Putin, one-point-of-view information sharing; ensuring the brain would atrophy again. Without multiple sources, without encouragement to think, Russians are becoming mouthpieces for the State. And Kristi's words pointed to present-day America. With the plethora of sound bite broadcasting—e.g., Fox and Breitbart News—the dark web, and smartphones that skip information from phone to phone like pebbles across a stream, what are people retaining? What are children learning that will develop their long-term memories necessary for thinking? What information will people have to make informed decisions?

Lying

"It will be very difficult for me to go back to the Soviet Union. That's why, unlike my colleagues here, I have not bought goods. No shoes, no clothes, no nothing. Why? They will look at me. They will never forgive me if I have these things, the same way they will never forgive Raisa Gorbachev that she has something better than they do. So, I won't do it."

Tasha Ledyovna, a thirty-five-year-old exchange teacher to the US from Yaroslavl, took me aside in New York to share her sentiments. Her soft voice corroborated her gentle round Slavic features, a trace of the Steppes in her eyes.

Her words reminded me of the pressure for Soviet flats to appear uniform. It was as if everyone had lined up at the one store that sold one type of sofa bed, dark wardrobes, faux-oriental wall rugs, mini four-burner stoves, white refrigerators, and a formica-top, metal framed table with chairs. Tatyana's comment about Raisa Gorbachev made sense. I'd heard frequently from Soviet friends expressing disgust with anyone who strived to have more than others. It was as if they lived like crabs in the bottom of a cage, and when the food ran out, no crab would allow any other to escape to find more. The Communist ideology lived in the collective psyche in which people persevered.

She was one of fifteen Soviet exchange teachers I'd chaperoned for AFS in New York City in November 1987 before they returned home. During our private conversation, I asked her why she struggled to speak the truth in her life and the role the school played.

"Lying begins in the schools," she said forlornly. "That was the main reason I hated my school. The teachers tell students what they have to tell them. They are not interested in what they think. The teacher is interested only if the children use the right words. Children become accustomed to saying the right words, not the real words. And that's how they become two different people."

She paused, her intensity evident. I waited. "I am a teacher of literature. I have to check all the essays of the students' entrance exams for the university. I hate to read them because none of them write what they really think. They write what they are supposed to think—from formulas, not from the heart. You cannot see what kind of person they are. They learn this from their teachers who cotton to the system and believe it is right. This is the worst thing about our educational system. It lies."

"What about the organization of Young Pioneers? Is that a lie too?"

"Sure it's a lie, because the Pioneer goal is not to develop yourself, your own opinion. Its goal is to accept the system, to accept the opinion of all the rest of the people and not try to think deeply about what's going on. You may have heard the story of Pavlic Morozov. Pavlic discovered his father was against collectivization and turned him in to Party authorities and the KGB. His father was arrested and killed—shot. When Pavlic's uncles found out that Pavlic had betrayed his own father, they shot him. Now Pavlic's considered a Pioneer hero. I believe such stories are very dangerous, because they are trying to make fanatics out of our kids."

Her voice quivered as she leaned closer, "I hate fanaticism on any scale. Fanatics have been dangerous throughout history. We are trying to tell the truth now in our country, but we still say one thing in company and another thing in a close circle of friends. We are in a system that makes us say the wrong things, to behave in a wrong way. We can't resist it, so we have to find a way around."

"Are you willing to lie?"

"Sometimes yes . . ."—she frowned—"even if I hate to do it. Unfortunately, it is true. People would never forgive me if I decided to try to tell the truth, because not one of them is free enough, brave enough to tell the truth themselves. When people see someone brave enough to tell the truth, they sit and wait for someone to beat him." She took a deep breath. "I hate it in our society. I hate it in our country! I hate it in myself. The whole society is raised in this way—not to tell the truth."

Tasha revealed a third leg to explain the underpinnings of Soviet school behavior: *podskazka*, *shparlgaka*, and now the lying. She understood—perhaps more so from her visit to the States—that Soviet textbooks repeated lies about the US: its rampant homelessness, the depraved family life in poor towns, and the USSR's initiatives for peace while the US pushed for war. Each leg reinforced the other. Each was embedded in a cruel system that rewarded conformity, consistency, and continuity.

DID MY PRESENCE in Soviet schools allow me to discover its truths? Were people honest with me, as Tasha Ledyovna had been in New York? Through my countless conversations with teachers, students, and friends in flats, in parks, on sidewalks, in cafés, and in my hotel room, I believe that I was finding my way further and further inside the *matryoshka*, inside the truths of Soviet society.

I chose not to behave like the American who knew better, who claimed to know the right way to educate. I invited my Soviet colleagues to trust me. I resided in the cult of the Soviet collective with all its prompting, cheating—and lying, and I even prompted once when I was observing a lesson from the back of the room. And I was aware that the American cult of the individual had its own foibles, particularly the fierce competitiveness that led to plagiarism, cheating—and lying.

Those who practice these things are destined to pass them on. Recalling that physics student thirty years before Gorbachev who marked the corner of an exam card for his friend, Russian students today pass on the practice—only now via electronics. I learned of the most intriguing *shparlgaka* from a recent telephone conversation with Sasha, the daughter of a teacher friend and recent Russian high school graduate:

"Students who live in earlier time zones (there are nine in Russia as of 2010) pass on answers to friends to the east . . . . And *podska-zka* continues its presence in a slightly different form. In my school, pupils would whisper after the teacher asked a question before one of them would stand to answer."

One generation follows another. What was considered to be Russian in Soviet times continues in the new Russia today. And the pattern of teachers delivering from the front of the room in both our countries might appear similar, but inside each culture teachers aim to achieve their respective beliefs.

X
INTERNATIONAL PIONEER CAMP

It is expressed by the knight in chess, which when moved, the opponent does not know where it will land: we think one way, say another, and do the third.

Pavel Kozhevnikov, letter, June, '15

"**Y**es, we certainly can and will do the laundry. The city has been kind enough to lend us a washing machine big enough to wash clothes for 150 people—easy to take care of your 75 students and guests. Our Ludmilla will take care of it."

And sort all the clothes? I pondered.

WASHING EVERYONE'S CLOTHES was yet one more of a myriad of bureaucratic follies facing Pavel Kozhevnikov, the director of Pioneer camp, Zhemchuzhina (a pearl) in Alma-Ata, Kazakhstan, 2500 miles east of Moscow on a border with China. Pavel was responsible for hosting international delegations of American, Japanese, and Soviet high-schoolers and their counselors. As we Americans debarked from our plane at Alma-Ata's airport, a short man in a blue suit and tie, hair disheveled, smiled as he greeted us, revealing a gold tooth in his upper jaw.

"Welcome to Alma-Ata, the city of apples. We are glad that you are here. I am Pavel Kozhevnikov, the director of our camp." He handed Gail Wilson, one of the American counselors, a bouquet of beauteous flowers, as Ed Porter, another counselor, and our nineteen wide-eyed students and I looked on. We immediately recognized Pavel's exhausted energy; he must have been working for weeks before we arrived.

It had been two years since I last stepped on Russian soil. AFS invited me to be a counselor to the US students. I would be returning to a country I cherished, another chance to probe behind the red veil and perhaps deeper into the *matryoshka*.

Unlike my previous trips, when I had been divorced and unattached, I arrived in a different frame of mind. I was now in a nearly year-long, live-in relationship with Kathleen, whom I'd met at a Halloween party after my last trip to the Soviet Union as a tour leader.

Another difference for this trip: My mother had been in and out of the hospital with lung cancer. But the invitation to Kazakhstan was too intriguing to pass up. Traveling to a different part of the Soviet Union far from Moscow, being a counselor to high-schoolers, and collecting new material for my book was irresistible. One month there and then home. That should work.

The first couple of days at Zhemchuzhina were low key, allowing us to adjust to the hot, dry continental climate. Students from the three countries asked a myriad of questions of one another and learned each other's names—especially the Japanese and Americans; the Soviets, a mixture of Russians and Kazakhs, held back. Gail and Pavel seemed to pay special attention to each other.

On the evening of our third day, Pavel arranged an opening ceremony. Our Kazakh hosts wore bright red-and-yellow festive costumes—elegant portrayals of their Mongol heritage. The Japanese dressed somewhat alike, many in kimonos; the Americans appeared more informal. As master of ceremonies, Pavel, a teacher acting as a bureaucrat in his handsome pressed white suit, behaved like a crazy Russian with a big heart, an eye for sentimentality, his charisma infectious.

We soon became privy to Pavel's decision-making. But we didn't know until much later that he had been in daily conflict with the lady director of the camp, who was, to say the least, a corrupt bureaucrat; we never saw her. In the evening, we met with him and his staff: sullen André Voinovich, his driver; tall Larissa Ivanova, the vivacious sports organizer; and youthful Lena Mikhailovna and Irina Dmitrievna, Russian teachers who were his assistants. Irina, the younger, more attractive, and appearing somewhat melancholic, was intriguing. Her shyness seemed to be hiding something, something I wanted to look for.

We would discuss plans for the next day and week: excursions, banquets, national cultural days, a school visit, and home stays. Pavel's immediate boss, Bulat, lingered in the background and did little more than drink vodka—we later learned he was KGB.

Pavel appeared remarkably open, yet his actions frequently perplexed us. Sometimes what he promised or intended did not materialize. Something as simple as pepper shakers, forty-five of them, on the tables for the Japan-day lunch—all empty! Or the cheese for the American-day grilled-cheese luncheon that disappeared until mysteriously found! He was never at a loss to explain—and we accepted what he had to say. His humor was irrepressible.

Pavel was everywhere. "We will arrange everything," was his mantra. Because he had a devoted staff—"my girls"—often by some miracle, without fanfare, things got done. And one morning when I missed breakfast, a tray appeared in my room! I became a believer.

Pavel's actions reflected a Russian proverb, which he later shared in a letter. "It is expressed by the knight in chess, which when moved, the opponent does not know where it will land; we think one way, say another, and do the third." Pavel was operating inside a system foreign to us. Yet we felt its impact. And he was allowing us to become privy to another layer of the *matryoshka*.

NINE DAYS INTO the camp, Pavel led us on a five-day excursion into the dry Kazakh desert to Chimkent (now Shymkent), first by train and then by bus, to visit the ancient town of Turkestan and the Shrine of Ahmed Yasavi. But none of us knew where we were going or why.

Our train rumbled into the night. Shortly after supper, an attendant passed through each carriage carrying bed sheets and demanding one ruble from each of us. "Why wasn't this taken care of in the ticket?" some of us asked; another reminder of Soviet bureaucracy. By then, we were barely into our nine-and-a-half-hour trip; it was a hot, dry train, the compartments impossible to sleep in. The kids were beside themselves.

Rachel, lively and caring among her peers, wound her way from carriage number two to carriage number five to ask me to come to help Jill, who'd been suffering from a severe headache for nearly two hours. Jill was our spirited Kansan, a sunflower if ever there was one. Rachel gave her aspirin, but it did not help. I arrived to find her crying. I instinctively put her head between my hands and remained quiet. By the time I'd let go, I was as surprised as Jill that she was better—and even more surprised to be experiencing pain in both arms. I'd been a conduit, certainly not a healer. Teaching let me know that I could make a difference, but I would never know how or when. With Jill that night, I'd responded to her headache in the only way I could envision.

THE NEXT MORNING—the heat still oppressive—we boarded three brown, tired camel-buses with bulging fenders, broken bumpers, sticky vinyl seats, dirty windows, and no A/C. I made it a point to sit in the front next to the attractive, melancholic Irina Dmitrievna. I'd been scoping her out since Pavel introduced us; her eyes lingered on

mine while resting her hand on her cheek, gently sliding it through
her hair before looking away. During our first days, she seemed to be
playing hard to get, which drew me in to want to spend time alone
with her, to look into her eyes, to have a conversation, to come to
know her. Whenever I tried to break the ice—her English was excellent—she would shy away and find an excuse to retreat to one of her
friends. Now we would be next to each other for who knew how long.

We sat quietly at first as the buses ambled onto a narrow, two-
lane asphalt strip with no median line and no shoulders which led
into the baked countryside of southern Kazakhstan. Passing tractors
and trucks, the drivers seemed to play chicken with oncoming traffic
and havoc with our hearts. After an awkward silence, Irina turned
to me, her eyes looking into mine. Again, it was that Russian melancholic look, the one that speaks without words, the one that Elena
Vladimovna in Leningrad had first shown me. No language, just the
lingering look, longer than when we had met. As the bus rambled
into the desert, I would wait to pursue the meaning of that look and
instead stuck to light conversation about life at the camp, but occasionally our hands touched. Neither of us pulled away.

After an hour or so and repeated stalling, our bus sputtered and
died. Sweating in the dry air, we were parched and uncomfortable,
some of us becoming cranky. We watched the other buses disappear
over the horizon. Soon they returned, perhaps because our bus was
carrying cases of mineral water. While we waited for the drivers to
make repairs, students started to grumble. Pavel broke out the cases.
When we opened the bottles, the contents skyrocketed like cham-
pagne! We struggled to quench our thirst with water as hot as breakfast tea.

Once our driver restarted the engine, our bus ambled on for
another hour past the ancient town of Turkestan, past our intended
destination to the shrine. Pavel's raspy voice shouted from the back.

"By now, everyone, we are late for lunch. We need to reach the wonderful Greek restaurant, Kosmos, near the next town, Kentau. Please be patient."

At Kosmos, I sat at a table with my students; Irina sat with her Russian colleagues. It was some of the best food I've tasted in a Soviet restaurant, especially the *pelmeni*, delicious Siberian dumplings composed of small portions of minced beef and onions wrapped in thin, unleavened dough and perfectly boiled. And we were treated to hot borscht and cold Pepsi, both of which Russians told me they prefer lukewarm.

They said that the ice-cold drinks would chill the throat and bring on sickness, though I watched people eat ice cream—and in the morning on the way to work! As for the rest of us, cold Pepsi was a respite from heat. I asked Irina if she knew the temperature outside. Pavel told her it was already 46° Celsius (112° Fahrenheit). Thank God it was desert dry heat!

After lunch, we headed back toward Turkestan to the shrine, which lay on the famed Silk Trade Route extending from China to Europe. It was the most magnificent mosque of medieval Turkistan, a religious center of the Moslem world and the largest mosque in Central Asia—a rectangular form topped by a huge dome sheathed in front with blue brick, 130 feet high and a copula 60 feet across containing more than thirty halls and rooms inside.

As we approached, the mosque rose like an apparition out of the vast flatland. Getting off the sweltering buses, we took a long pathway to its massive door into the cool air beneath its lofty dome, a welcome respite from the heat. After a half hour, we were about to leave, but Kumi insisted on one more picture—a Japanese habit—in front of the mosque. She smiled with her shoulder-length dark hair, red T-shirt, black Bermudas, and flip-flops; and I smiled as well in tan corduroy shorts, San Francisco T-shirt, Red Sox hat, black camera bag, and Birkenstocks.

We boarded our bus, sitting again on sticky, hot vinyl seats, and headed back toward Chimkent on the same narrow road, a weaving mirage-ribbon-pattern built by Soviet engineers and sunstruck construction workers. Our cold Pepsi and the cool dome receded into a distant memory. Thankfully, the sun was beginning to move behind us.

In the late afternoon, with little relief from the heat, our bus, slowed by its hesitant engine, pulled into a parking lot next to the other two, where Pavel had said that we would find water for swimming and a place to eat. We ambled down a winding, narrow path to a small shack selling *Vinnie Pookh* sodas. Eager to quench our parched thirst, I bought some for Irina, and for Ida, Jason, Nicole, Kumi, Tanya, and me. But the bottles were as hot as the mineral water we'd had in the morning. After a sip, I dumped the rest on the ground.

Hearing voices, we followed the path beyond the kiosk, which opened to a wide river with shallow water rushing over rocks and surrounded by lush green vegetation. There our comrades were frolicking and splashing below a high barren canyon cliff. It looked like a movie set. They hollered for us to join them.

In my corduroy shorts, I slipped into the cool waters to venture across to the swifter current. We lay on our stomachs with our hands touching the bottom to guide us as we floated into deeper waters. Floating heads, bobbing, babbling, laughing, giggling. Three cultures expressing joy: Miki, Hiroko, and Shinko; Sofia, Dima, and Tanya; and Jason, Jill, and Rachel, each in their own language. Jill was exuberant, her headache gone. I caught Irina watching me frolic—and I think she noticed me checking her out.

After an hour, Pavel called us to supper. Taking a couple more runs, more splashing, playful pushing—mostly the Americans—we left the rushing waters. In fewer than ten minutes my corduroy shorts were bone dry.

We ate in a Kazakh *yurta* set up with long tables. Our meal: my favorite Russian salad made from diced potato, peas, egg, and mayonnaise; *shashlik*, a form of shish kebob made with lamb with unleavened bread and tomato sauce; *blinis*, thin unleavened pancakes; and ice cream for dessert—and cold beer for the group leaders.

We were in a piece of heaven. No other way to explain it. We were only twenty kilometers from Chimkent where the buses left earlier that morning. On one of the hottest days of the summer, we traveled 330 kilometers to find a place to swim and eat. Pavel took us on what seemed like an endless journey: rides in tired buses with broken air conditioning, a lunch at a Greek restaurant, a short visit to an ancient mosque, culminating in a joyful swim in a swift river and a beyond-delicious supper in a splendid Kazakh yurta.

We had lived through what I thought was a useless type of suffering, a self-inflicted suffering, an unnecessary suffering. By the time we arrived at the river, I was at a loss as to what to expect and resigned to accept whatever fate would bring. Perhaps that's how Russians felt about their lives. I was discovering a satisfaction, a joy, Russian style. Without the painful, sweltering heat of the 330 kilometer bus ride, without enduring the 112 degrees, the swim in the fast current would not have become the memory it has—nor would the Greek restaurant Kosmos, the ancient Turkestan mosque, or supper in the yurta.

My Russian friends savored small pleasures in life, so commonplace that most Americans would not recognize them. A gala evening with friends—rare for them and only after days of preparation—with meat, vegetables, salad, bread, cheese, along with vodka *and* cognac around a crowded table in a living room or the bedroom of a tiny apartment. A walk in a park in the sunshine in the November cold. Or discovering a roll of toilet paper in a shop, or finding a bunch of bananas.

Other simple pleasures, such as a conversation after school in a sparse, dirty, cockroach café; the joy of getting peace pins from Americans; the glee of landing a pair of jeans from the States. Whichever these pleasures—and countless others—they appeared as gifts to help break up the struggles with constant scarcity. "We are always thinking about what we will find in the shops," a Russian friend said to me.

In comparison with the average Russian at that time, the average American was used to life's little details working out. But suffering has resided deep in Russian history. Depravity has been embedded. While the American and Japanese students became restless when our bus stalled, the Soviets remained calmer. It was as if they expected that something would go wrong. Pavel, obviously under extreme pressure, kept his cool.

Pavel later explained in a letter that the trip had not been his idea. A Kazakh deputy from Chimkent insisted that "Americans see the treasure of Kazakh soil," the Shrine of Ahmed Yasavi. Had Pavel described the itinerary to us counselors, we likely would have refused to go. Our not going would have been, in Pavel's words, referring to Kazakh pride, "a spite in the nationalist face." The swim in the Arys River and the party in the yurta was his idea. A Russian bureaucratic ploy became a remarkable journey.

LIFE IN AND around the camp, though less eventful than the Chimkent trip, was nonetheless memorable. Three cultures of high schoolers and counselors mingled every day. We played volleyball and basketball in the outdoor pavilion and softball on the field next to it, and took hikes into the surrounding hills to view the city below. We wandered among Communist slogans, images of Lenin, a Pavlic Morozov statue (I recalled my conversation about Pavlic with Tasha Ledeyova in New York), and ate tasty Kazakh-Russian food.

Pavel was a bottomless resource. He worked tirelessly every day to make the camp work. He planned excursions to museums, sports arenas, a Pioneer palace, his school N° 22, and other sites in the city. We celebrated each culture: a Japan day, an American day, and a Soviet-Kazakh day. In the late evenings, vodka and cognac enhanced staff conversations.

Pavel's closing ceremony proved equal to the opening. Kazakhs in their colorful dress demonstrated some of their traditions, the Japanese expressed their polite thanks, and five Americans wrote and sang a final song to The Crystals' "Da Doo Ron Ron."

WHAT DOES ONE take from a month's immersion into a separate world? A Soviet camp on the border of China, embedded inside an old Kazakh culture, far from the Moscow web. Pavel, the Russian bureaucratic knight, imparted his will in a situation fraught with fractures. Despite challenges, he and his staff exhibited kindness and warmth—traits I'd come to expect from Russians. We spent far more time laughing than being frustrated with what was not working. That seemed to be the Russian way, something I'd seen many times before. And the kids bonded across three cultures.

John Sevenau, by far the tallest, has posted numerous items on Facebook from that time. It was obvious that Zhemchuzhina Pioneer camp had become a personal sojourn for all of us. We immersed in the camp's culture: Kazakhs, Russians, Japanese, and Americans. In this setting, I became hyper aware, yet again, of the pulls and tugs of Soviet life.

The original idea of an international camp on Soviet soil appeared in Leonid Brezhnev's time before Gorbachev, only to stumble through Soviet bureaucracy and emerge near the end of the Gorbachev era. Regardless of its source, it was yet another top-down, Party-imposed idea, designed for political gain: to show the world another example of a Soviet effort for peace. Pavel and his people put their best feet forward to impress us with their way of life. But the interactions of high school kids and their chaperones from three countries would make it their own domain. Under the canopy of Zhemchuzhina, we were who we would have been anywhere. Maybe that had been Pavel's intention all along—one he never told his bosses about.

BEING YET AGAIN amid Russians, I was searching for something more. This land of "a riddle wrapped in a mystery inside an enigma" was enticing me to reevaluate who I was and what I wanted in life. I had been a teacher, husband, and parent who moved through phases of my life with gusto. After meeting Kathleen, I plunged into our relationship and was picturing possibly becoming a stepparent to her kids. Now I was in a republic on the edge of the Soviet Union in a summer camp as a counselor, which was less demanding than teaching. It was giving me time to pause, to reconsider how I should walk my path.

A revealing moment came one afternoon in a conversation with Stephen "Woo-man" Rhee, a high schooler from New York, when we were sitting on a bench near the ball field.

"Don't you agree, Frank-man," he asked with a twinkle in his eye, "right field is where the best of baseball happens?"

"Yes, Woo-man, I have thought about that since I was ten years old at summer camp. My younger brother was our centerfielder and lead-off hitter. The counselor—I forget his name—put me in right field and batting ninth. Batting ninth, the worst hitter. Right field, where players 'go out to pasture,' where balls rarely arrive. Plenty of time for contemplation."

"I played right field too, Frank-man. I can see you and me placing our weight on the left leg, the right foot turned slightly outward, hands and glove held low at the top of the left thigh, and head slightly cocked. Time to contemplate."

"I know that stance, Woo-man. It's baseball's Rodin!"

We were two Americans in a place far from home. Reaching into a space dear to both of us, I recovered a memory. In a letter to Stephen the following September, I wrote:

Greetings from right field, where life gains perspective, where truth enters the heart, where the soul mingles with the mind.

For the two of us, right field has been our modus operandi, our frame of reference.

That afternoon, our conversation rekindled a way of reflecting that I would evoke in my later years in the classroom and in my life.

IN OUR LAST week, Pavel arranged homestays, his idea for us to experience Kazakh home life. I accepted Irina Dmitrievna's invitation to stay with her in her flat. By this time Irina and I had discussed the possibility that I might return in January to teach English at her school, N° 15. She suggested that if I stayed with her, we could meet the director and some of her colleagues, who were eager for me to come.

My first thought was that staying with Irina would solidify my chances for teaching in her school, something I knew I would never forget. It never occurred to me—my naiveté showing up again—that Irina might be hoping we'd develop a relationship, and even more so, that I might be her ticket out of the Soviet Union. Since the Chimkent trip, we'd been spending more time together at the camp. Not a day passed that we didn't have a personal encounter, but we were very discreet. We would sit together at the same table at some meals, sit next to each other at times to watch events at the camp, and ride together on bus trips to venues that Pavel had arranged. It seemed whenever we had an opportunity, we'd exchange glances and let them linger. I felt pulled into her aura and wanting to touch her hair, hold her hand, caress her.

As the weeks passed, my thoughts about home and my relationship with Kathleen grew dimmer. Was I letting myself be lured into a layer of the *matryoshka* that I was not ready for? The rest of the world seemed to be slipping into the ether. Sometimes I would only see Irina when we were surrounded by others. I'd learned about the lure of melancholic Russian women with Elena Vladimovna. Now it was biting me again.

The homestay would be a test of my character. In past trips, I'd traveled alone, unattached. Not this time. Back home, Kathleen and her two kids were waiting for me. The first evening of the homestay, Irina and I dined with students at another home. I consumed about eight vodka toasts, shouting "Kampai!" (Japanese for "Cheers!") each time. I drank far more vodka than I'd been used to. After dinner, I insisted on telephoning other homes to see how other kids were doing. Irina and I bade farewell to our hosts and ambled—as best as we could—to her three-room, quite modern flat.

We reeled our way up to the second floor, fumbled with the keys to open the door, stepped inside, and fell onto the couch, her head on my lap. We decided to have another drink, not that we needed one. We then opened up the sofa bed in her living room and laid out sheets and a blanket. She looked at me and said, "Good night, Frank," her eyes lingering yet again.

"Good night, Irina" I replied, not letting go of her look.

She turned to go into her bedroom, a slow stroll that seemed to last forever. She left the door open. I fumbled while undressing, flinging my clothes onto the floor and putting on my pajamas, I slipped into the sofa bed. I had a hard time settling, partly from its narrowness, partly from the drinking—and not wanting to be alone, or wanting . . .

"Are you all right, Frank?" said Irina from the bedroom.

"Yes, but I'm missing you."

"Why don't you come in here, and I'll help you fall asleep."

Whoa, I said to myself. In bed with her! I'm not sure . . . I am sure . . . . I lay down beside her. We lay on top of the covers. I felt a sense of privacy surrounding us, of being in a place no one would ever know. My heart was pounding, my body breathlessly aroused. After a long quiet, I moved closer to her, our bodies touching, not moving. Before I knew it, we were making love, very slowly, very slowly. We were in a space we'd not talked about but that both of us wanted. I stayed for the night and in her bed for the other two nights for the homestay.

THE DAY WE were to leave the camp, the final reckoning, the banquet, I woke up and looked out from my balcony. Below in the grass was a tethered sheep.

"Why is the sheep there?" I asked Ed.

"It will be slaughtered and served at the banquet later in the morning. It's the favorite feast for Kazakhs." I recalled images of banquets with a sheep's head as the centerpiece, a practice I thought belonged in the Middle Ages. But we're in Mongol country in the twentieth century!

We gathered cross-legged on the ground on woven mats around an elaborate red-clothed banquet area filled with fruit, vegetables, and the sheep's head in front of our hosts. By the time we arrived, we'd already had our share of vodka. We listened to a Kazakh official say his farewell—Pavel translated. He wanted to show us his best. Being a red-meat-eating culture, the sheep was their food of choice.

At the conclusion of the host's speech, as a token of respect he offered us the delicacy of the sheep's eye, which he would be honored to have us eat. I panicked! My God, eat a sheep's eye? My excuse came quickly.

"I'm sorry. I am a teacher. I do not eat pupils."

Pavel translated my comment, and after a pause, brief laughter and hesitant smiles from our hosts. Ed, having had extra vodka, dropped both of the eyes into his mouth, dipped his fingers into the brain, lukewarm and uncooked—and ate it!

XI
INVOKING THE PERSONAL

Now I can hear and enjoy the music of my soul. I know I'm gonna miss you. I'll never forget our lessons. I hope someday you'll come back like Mary Poppins with the west wind but with the help of Pan Am. Thank you for being so kind, so patient, friendly, and warm to us.

Maya, April 1991

When I returned home from Alma-Ata and stepped off the train in White River Junction, Vermont, Kathleen was waiting. We looked at each other. Hoping for a hug, I stepped toward her. But she held back.

"Hello, Kathleen."

"Hi."

That was it. She turned toward her car. I gathered my suitcases and followed her. On the way to her house, we hardly spoke. How did she know? I wondered. But I had no need to ask. I knew the moment she saw my face, she knew I'd been bad. Yes, I had, and now I was feeling guilty. And I deserved it. We both knew at that moment that I'd broken a trust and would be paying for it.

I slept on her couch that night. The next morning, I found my suitcases by the front door. I went back to my room at the home of a different Quaker Friend who had offered it in exchange for doing chores, this time scraping layers of paint off the back of her barn. I again set up my Mac and continued to write. A couple of days later, Kathleen told me that she had moved my stuff out of her house.

I was devastated, as if tossed into a barren desert. But I didn't moan and groan to anyone. This was between Kathleen and me; it was my doing and I needed to undo it. I would regroup and try to find a way back into our relationship. Irina had been an interim affair—not for her, as I later discovered, but for me.

Meanwhile, I anguished over whether to secure a visa to teach at School № 15 in January, four months away. I decided to be open to whatever fate would bring. Were I to return to Alma-Ata, Kathleen would believe that she no longer counted in my life. I didn't feel that way, but no words from me would likely convince her otherwise. But not to go would mean missing the unique opportunity to teach Russian children three time zones from Moscow and Leningrad. Would these children be similar? Would schooling in a different republic have its own idiosyncrasies? Would I be able to be myself as a teacher? But surely it would mean more material for my book.

I decided not to decide, revisiting an old avoidance behavior. I would apply for a visa and if I got it—a fifty-fifty chance at best—I would go. If not, I would stay and begin to rebuild my life. Besides, I was running out of my small savings. I needed to find a job. I was eager to return to the classroom, to have an opportunity to share what I had come to know about the Russian people. And I would be closer to my mother who was seriously ill in South Carolina.

Kathleen was dating other men. We would talk occasionally, but I made little progress. I spent most of my time working on my book, scraping the back of the barn for several hours a day, and, in the evenings, watching Red Sox baseball at a local bar run by Yankee aficionados.

In December, the visa arrived. Fate had delivered the unexpected. I hesitated to accept it. Going to Alma-Ata would likely close the door to Kathleen and would take me farther from my mother. But the temptation to be an American teacher in Kazakhstan for three months was irresistible.

Two and a half weeks later, on January 17, I flew to Leningrad, the day the US invaded Kuwait. I had no idea this was happening.

AFTER I'D SPENT a week with my friend Misha Baushev, Irina met me as planned at the Moskovsky train station to escort me to Alma-Ata. We'd hardly communicated since I'd last seen her. But because my coming was her "baby," she had the right to bring the American to her school. Dressed in a long black coat, her straight short dark hair peeking below a wool cap, her brown eyes lit up, and in a soft voice, she said shyly, "I am so glad to see you, Frank. I can't wait until we're together in my flat—and have you meet my students. They are waiting for you."

I was queasy with the knowledge of what lay behind Irina's words. The arrangement for me to come to teach in Alma-Ata also meant that she had the right to host me in her flat. I was nervous about the arrangement, but decided that I could stay there and not jeopardize my outside chances to be with Kathleen again. It was a risk, and I knew Kathleen would know if I rekindled my affair.

For three days Irina and I sat beside each other in a Spartan coach. Our Trans-Siberian train steamed through the snowy landscape of rural Russia and through the Ural Mountains, passing one rustic station after another. Each displayed its statue of Lenin, the dead Lenin-god welcoming us, his right hand often held high. Irina brought sandwiches, fruit, and sweets that lasted for most of the trip. She must have sensed my constraint. I was lamenting that I'd made the wrong decision about coming. I kept thinking about Kathleen and realized that I cared even more deeply for her than I had been willing to admit. To avoid having conversations on the train, I read most of the time. On Wednesday, January 30, we arrived in Alma-Ata.

The next day, Irina and I walked from her flat to the school. When we had settled into her three-room apartment the evening before, we were cordial with one another, but it was clear I was not behaving like the Frank she expected. Walking to her school, we could focus on the business of my becoming a teacher, which made it easier between us. On the way, she explained that School N° 15 had 1,700 students attending in two shifts; the fifth, sixth, and seventh forms met from two to seven.

As we approached, I said, "My goodness, Irina, your school is huge. It is the biggest I've seen in the Soviet Union!"

"Yes, it is very big. But I hope you'll like it."

We stepped into a barren vestibule where I immediately felt an emptiness of spirit. Where is the energy? Where's the hustle and bustle I'd felt in Leningrad and Moscow? Will I feel at home? Why am I here?

"Welcome, Frank," said Rima Ivanovna, the director, reaching to shake my hand, her hair in a bun, her round face alight with a warm smile, her blue suit neatly pressed. She commanded a presence without arrogance.

"We've been waiting for you," she said in the now familiar stilted British English. "Come sit." She gestured to Irina and me to take the two wooden chairs with seat pads across from her desk. "You must be tired from your long trip. I am eager for you to work in our school. I have arranged for your pay. Elena Nikolaevich, our English Department leader, will give you your schedule. Irina Dmitrievna will be your host. Again, welcome, Frank."

Once done with these details, Rima Ivanovna proudly recounted that she'd returned recently from a two-week trip to the States with Pavel Kozhevnikov, the director from the camp, who was finishing his teaching at School N° 22 before joining Gail in Colorado—no surprise, as they had become an item at the camp. She asked questions and offered few opinions in stark contrast to Elvira Nikolaevna's pontifications at School N° 185. I sensed that she did not want to form a relationship. Not in the cards, nor was it my intention.

She scheduled weekly meetings with three different groups of teachers, but we only met a couple of times. The school had different levels of English. I mostly taught the "intensive" groups, which met every day, their English comparable to students in Leningrad and Moscow. The weaker groups had English only once or twice a week; they were more hesitant in front of their first American, and I had to pull teeth to get them to talk. I wondered how the school sorted the kids.

In my first week, it was as if I were back in Leningrad or Moscow. I saw the same blue- and-brown uniforms, red scarves, desks in pairs in rows, and the same texts. I observed the familiar teaching methodology: children raising their right hands at the elbows, standing to answer questions, the whispering, sitting with permission—and the chaotic buzz in the corridors at breaks. In my classes, I invoked the routine teaching from Soviet texts. But I was surprised to be feeling less enamored with my teaching, although the teachers and children might not have thought so. They were enjoying the American, but I was looking for more.

And students vocalized the usual propaganda about America, regurgitating State TV's *Vremya*. But I sensed a latent curiosity from them wanting to probe beneath the known, especially the older ones. I felt as if I were acting as a gardener, turning the earth over for them for the first time. Together we might reside inside the *matryoshka,* in a garden where we might form deeper relationships. Certainly I was not the mini-mythic superhero American I'd been in my first days at School N° 185. Instead, more like a tiller of life, a tiller of minds. If so, was I up to it? Was I capable?

Although I met with the younger children for only one class

(it *was* a huge school), I would try to learn all of their first names. Once I established a rhythm in all my classes, I employed humor, mostly puns with middle- and high-schoolers, admittedly difficult in a second language. In Leningrad, I had discovered that being "the funny American" brought me closer to my students, especially the younger ones. I wrote in a letter home to Kathleen:

> *Today, I asked the children in a third-form class dressed in their blue and brown Octobrist uniforms, the girls with their white aprons, if they knew my name. Five students in the front row, one after another said Frank. So I wrote "Frank, Frank, Frank, Frank, Frank" on the board and said that was my name. From there we had many laughs.*
>
> *In the next group, also third-formers, I asked the same question. One boy raised his hand, jumped up, and said, "I don't know." So I adopted that name for the lesson! Later, I asked some of them, "How old are you?" Immediately after that question, I pointed to a girl, "What is your name?" She said "Nine," so I wrote it as her name on the board.*
>
> *Before that, a girl was laughing so hard, she could not say her name. So I smiled and put my tongue between my teeth as she had done and said that was her name. You can imagine what fun we are having.*

I wondered if my silliness might be pirating their ability to learn English. I was not doing drill-and-kill lessons, which I observed my Soviet colleagues engaged in day after day. Yet invoking humor with primary children energized them to speak English. We never slipped into Russian; I did not know the language.

After a lesson with one second-form group, I wrote in the same letter:

They run up to me in the corridor and hug me—ten at a time! I almost cry. I can barely speak their language, and they are just beginning to learn English, and yet we know each other! I am astonished at the warmth I feel and share with children. I am blessed with the gift to be with them, to love them, to understand them. I believe I can be this way in my life. Children are my teachers. I learn so much from them.

LATER ONE MORNING in the second week, I walked into a fifth-form classroom and overheard boys lauding Arnold Schwarzenegger and Chuck Norris. Curious, I leaned toward one of them:

"Arnold Schwarzenegger, you say?"

He looked at me, dropped his eyes, and looked up again. "Yes, I like his movies."

"I like Chuck Norris," said another.

I stepped to the front of the class. "Why do you like these people?" There was a lapse while I took attendance—each child must be wondering why this teacher was asking for their opinions.

Dima, the shortest in the class, said, "I like the way they fight."

Alyosha, wide-eyed and alert, jumped up. "It's exciting!"

"I agree!" said Nicholas, nodding vigorously.

"Do any of you know what 'an eye for an eye' means?" Silence. "Have you ever heard of the saying: 'an eye for an eye makes the world blind'?" I took time to try to explain it using pantomime and wrote it on the board.

"How is that possible?" asked little Lena, her glasses slipping down her nose. "How can the world go blind?"

"Think about it for a moment, think about it . . . ."

MY TIME AT the Pioneer camp had affected me more than I realized. The "right-field" conversations with Woo-man rekindled my love of the philosophical and later the spiritual. I returned to Alma-Ata with a new desire to go into the deeper parts of teaching, the desire to seek meaning, to know my students' souls. Perhaps that's why I wanted to reenter the Soviet cocoon, a safe place for me to explore my own *matryoshka*. Despite the Communist Party's oppressive protocols on its society, I was finding space to be me—counterintuitive perhaps. I wonder how the Russians I respected, like Raisa Vladimirovna in Leningrad and Zoya Anatolyevna in Moscow, had been able to find that same space, or at least seemed to imply that they did.

One afternoon, teaching a lesson from the text to a seventh-form group, I began to sense how bored we were. And I was feeling a lack of impetus to be the front-and-center maestro, the entertainer, and yet again, the mini-mythic hero writ large. I stopped, turned and quietly wrote on the board Thich Nath Hanh's, "Wash the dishes to wash the dishes."

For nearly ten years I'd grappled with Hahn's aphorism. I had tried many times simply to wash the dishes without other thoughts or intentions. The previous Thanksgiving at a church where I'd fed the homeless and washed the dishes, I felt I might have succeeded, perhaps the only time in my life. Who knows? Perhaps a conversation with these Russian children might open them and me to understanding Hahn's wisdom.

Little Natasha, demure and quiet, sitting at the front, eyes on me, slowly mouthed Hanh's words. "What does this mean? It's silly!" Several others nodded.

"Okay, do any of you wash the dishes at home?"

"Yes," nearly everyone said.

"Okay, why do you wash the dishes?"

Dima almost stood in his seat. "I do them because my mother *tells* me to."

"So, again, why do the rest of you wash the dishes at home? Take time to think about it."

Mikhail, who had been sitting quietly in the back, suggested, "I do them to get them clean."

"Now we are getting somewhere." I smiled. "So you're told to wash them and you do it to get them clean. Do all of you agree?"

Most nodded yes.

Misha, somewhat overweight, said, "I do them as quickly as I can, so I can sit and watch TV."

"Okay, Misha, let's stop a minute. Let's look again and ask why I wrote this phrase on the board? What does it have to do with your life?" The room became quiet.

I took another approach and cautiously asked, "What if instead you consider washing the dishes not as a chore but as something fun? Would you think differently about doing them?"

I heard whispering, but no one spoke. Again I tried, "What if you were to see the act of washing dishes as something you liked to do? Would that make washing them any different?"

"What do you mean?" little Natasha asked.

I took a breath. "What I'm trying to show you is that to wash the dishes to wash the dishes means simply to wash them and not to do them for any other reason. Hanh calls this 'mindfulness'—I'll write it on the board. It means to be in the present, to act without thinking of the next thing you want to do. Simply choose to wash the dishes only to wash the dishes. Not as Misha said, to do them so he could watch TV."

Some seemed to be getting it. Others shook their heads. At least we were having a conversation—in English! As they prepared to leave, I offered a parting comment in a deliberate voice.

"You have many duties. Washing the dishes may be one of them. What if—think about this—what if you chose to do all your duties, every one of them, just to do them? Not for any other reason." The period ended and the class quietly gathered their materials. Little Natasha looked at me and shook her head as she walked out. So did

Dima. Mikhail grinned; I think he got it. And Misha said to me, "I *still* will do dishes so I can watch TV." The rest of the class appeared baffled, but most smiled at the American as they left.

Oh well, I thought, I tried. So much for better understanding Hanh's wisdom.

BY NOW IRINA and I had reached an impasse. We had been cordial for the most part, but the tension between us was clearly evident. She was missing the intimacy we'd had in the summer, and I was feeling guilty about having misled her. I slept on the sofa bed. Meanwhile, I wrote many long yellow legal-pad letters to Kathleen appealing for her to allow me back in her life, not knowing if the Soviet postal system would get them to her. (They did, but out of sequence.)

In addition to walking to school together on some days, Irina and I watched TV, visited with her friends, and invited them to come to us. Once we hosted a drunken party with her closest colleagues; my lewd behavior was not something to write home about, except that I did. I occasionally shared in the cooking; she taught me how to make *pelmeni.*

At school, we rarely saw each other. She did not observe my lessons, nor did I hers. I was surprised that she'd been willing to let me have her beloved 10B for many lessons. She was letting them go, knowing they would become my teachers. And with them I was feeling more drawn into myself, more comfortable being myself without fanfare, without the need to perform.

In the fourth week, we met again, perhaps for the third time. As I walked quietly into the classroom, they were eating apples, which Tanya had brought. She gave me one. Several asked if we could continue our discussion from a couple of days before about the afterlife. I had been curious at their responses, as it was the first time the subject had come up. I guess they were more than ready. (I turned on my cassette recorder in my pocket.)

Sasha, tall and insistent, raised his hand. "We only live one life. Science tells us that!"

Before anyone could respond, I held up an apple seed between my index finger and thumb. Twirling it around slowly, "Let's look at what happens to this seed." I drew a series of interlocking circles across the board to illustrate the cycle: apple seed, apple tree, apple, apple seed; apple seed, apple tree, apple, apple seed; apple tree, apple, etc.

"Where does the seed originate? I asked. Where is the 'first-first'? Where does the next seed come from?"

The room became still, except for muted crunching. Yulia, quiet at the last class, spoke first. "If I am good in this life, I'll reincarnate into another human being," she said assuredly. "If bad, I'll return as grass or something less. If I have no sin, then I'll go to paradise."

Some nodded. Yulia had grasped my questions but wanted to have her say, something she may well have been thinking about since our last class. Besides, I wanted to listen to what they had to say, rather than worrying about whether anyone would answer my query.

"So you've considered the role of reincarnation in your lives? I wouldn't think you've thought much about it." They had grown up under Communism after all.

"Oh yes, we talk about it a lot!" interjected the bright, inquisitive, dark-haired Luda.

Svetlana, often introspective, said, "I've thought a lot about religion, about heaven and hell, and about atheism, about not believing. I am coming to understand that I have a choice—we all have—as to what we believe and how we act. No one makes us say or do anything."

But Ira practically jumped out of his seat and bringing everyone back into the present said, "We have to act a certain way in school or we'll get into trouble!" He never failed to offer his opinion.

"Yes, I agree, Ira," Svetlana said in a calmer voice, "but as I said, in the end we *choose* what we do."

Tanya, whose broad smile permeated any room, shifted the discussion, and in her gentle manner, she said, "I always try to be kind to everybody, no matter who they are." Everyone perked up their ears. "I can't imagine being any different."

Lena, her dark hair resting near to her shoulders around her pensive eyes, quietly added, "Love is the most powerful force in the world."

The conversation probed and pondered the meaning of life in school, in society, and in the universe.

Sasha brought us back into the room just before the period ended and said quietly, "Tanya, you are the most polite person in our class."

She was.

After they left, I sat at my desk. I twirled my pencil and leaned back. Who have I been talking with? Surely these kids have not had lessons on the afterlife, on reincarnation. Yet they had spoken as if they intimately understood them. I took a long breath. I doubted that my students at home would have taken such a conversation seriously. Not in the classroom at least. I couldn't wait until the next time with 10B.

BY THE END of my first month, I'd ventured far from Soviet texts, from the heaviness of rote learning, from the hisses of prompting. Students were listening to one another, speaking their minds, and experiencing a deep sense of satisfaction. I was offering them the freedom to express themselves, to probe their deepest concerns, not simply to puppet texts. I never imagined that I might have been transgressing the curriculum. These students, especially 10B, sensed that I wanted to listen to them. I was the guest teacher from America. No one told me what I should do.

And their teachers became fascinated. Instead of observing their students regurgitating texts—admittedly boring—they would sit in the back having no expectation or opportunity to prompt. I would stand or sit depending upon the tenor of the conversation. For me, there was no turning back, no teaching from the texts for the older kids for the rest of my stay. I was discovering new insights about the lives of young Soviets lurking beneath the surface of the red veil of everyday school. No more "we pretend to learn while teachers pretend to teach." In another letter to Kathleen, I wrote:

> *I feel as though I am not only introducing different content into their English curriculum (which is boring to say the least), I am also having them think and speak in English, not easy in a second language, particularly when they've had little practice—some of their teachers don't speak it well. I introduce them to interesting and unusual ideas. The kids and I are becoming close. I feel their energy, light, and love! I feel connected now to the work I am doing, and I see its importance both for them and me.*
>
> *Perhaps I am the "catcher in the rye," but as a person, not as a "teacher helping to keep civilization from going over the cliff," as a New Hampshire reporter had portrayed me in Leningrad.*

I was on a roll, a new role in the classroom, becoming more aware of how my personal life informed my teaching. When teachers deliver materials dictated by others—prescribed curricula in the States, or designated texts in the Soviet Union—these materials often come between them and their students. And if a teacher chooses not to share about her personal self, students will often persist in wanting to know who she is. I was grateful to understand these values.

Many of School N° 15's older students were resisting the rigidity of the system. For one day a week, the school allowed them to choose what to wear in place of their blue Pioneer uniforms, white shirts, and red scarves. Perhaps this inkling of freedom emboldened their minds to explore new beliefs. And these young Kazakh Russians may have been sensing that the security of the Communism cocoon under Gorbachev was about to unravel. Whatever the reasons, I was the beneficiary of listening to their minds and hearts, to inner layers of their *matryoshkas*.

And I was being lured deeper into my *matryoshka*, into myself being my "self." I was moving behind my own veil, behind where others were seeing the "supposed-to-be-me." The person I desired to be. The person whose ego would keep me safe from others' seeing through me, from my admitting to my ego's fragility. It was a self-imposed veil that protected me from myself and from others.

From my childhood, I had been busy being Tommy Thoms, who'd stood naked at the front door of his family's inn; the kid who wanted to be known for his uniqueness; the adolescent who yearned to be someone important and recognized. I stepped into my first classroom seeking to be someone, a recognized teacher, a teacher-of-the-year. I strived to be unique in a profession that stressed that its members act and teach the same way.

ONE DAY WITH 10B I introduced "Just for Today," sayings I'd taken off my refrigerator the day before I left. After a few minutes, the students decided to translate them into Russian so they could better understand what to discuss.

Maya, who had been quiet, began, "This 'just for today' makes me think. I have trouble letting go of my anger." Her eyes moistened. "Perhaps it's because I hate having to do every day what teachers tell me. I am old enough to make my own decisions."

"I feel the same way," said Alyosha. "I'm tired of it!"

Tanya, tender Tanya who always appeared calm, offered a different perspective. "Why not admit we have the anger, but then put it aside; it's there but we don't have to act on it."

Luda, her best friend, said, "Tanya, you are an idealist, you always have been."

The perceptive and eager-to-talk Zhenya jumped in. "As for doing work honestly and diligently just for today, how can we do all our schoolwork without helping each other? Without Luda's help last spring, I would never have passed my chemistry exam. School does not allow for honesty." No one argued, and I wasn't surprised. Zhenya's words echoed those of many students I'd spoken too. She reaffirmed that *shparlgaka* was indeed a meme. There was no need to discuss it.

"How can I let go of worrying?" said Irene, who often appeared nervous. "I worry about my grandmother who is very sick. I worried about my dog when he was lost for several days. Worrying keeps me focused on my life."

Tanya leaned toward Irene. "Perhaps you could admit to your worry and then not let it bother you so much."

I joined the conversation. Taking a clue from Tanya, I said, "Why not tell yourself, Irene, that your worry is there; then take Tanya's advice and put it aside. Worrying about your grandmother does not help her—nor does it help you. Her sickness is not served by your worrying."

"I will have to think about that," Irene said quietly. "Maybe I can stop worrying just for today."

Whatever the topic, they took it as their own. They pondered Robert Frost's "The Road Not Taken" and "Stopping by Woods on a Snowy Evening." Another lively conversation emerged from "Life is difficult," the first sentence from Scott Peck's, *The Road Less Traveled*.[1] I would sit back and watch them stir in their seats as they contemplated on their own, seeking new perspectives, discovering insights as to how they might live their lives. We were building trust. No pretending.

I HARDLY SAW Irina at school. She chose to stay aloof because we were no longer close. Yet I imagined that she was well aware of what was happening in my classes. She had many close friends on the staff and was well liked. They knew how she was feeling. We did have some conversations about school, but they were not fertile for either one of us.

However, Irina surprised me when she planned a mid-March outing for 10B to the Zailiysky-Alatou mountains east of the city, a small mountain range set next to the giant Tien Shan range bordering China, which had snowcaps throughout the year. Snow fell in the city almost every day I was there, but only a dusting, never accumulating. Our trip was a memorable time.

The snow was deep, the air fresh, and the sun shining. We trudged up a trail on the Zailiysky-Alatou. Because it was impossible to walk down, students came with plastic bags filled with plastic bags. They showed me how to place them between our legs and slide down a path around curves against high banks shaped by previous sledders. Negotiating the winding trail challenged us to stay on our "sleds," occasionally careening deep into snow banks.

Once we reached bottom, we tossed each other into snow banks and had a snowball fight. After being hit with three snowballs in succession, I was laughing so hard I couldn't throw. And Irina was playing and laughing as well, conduct I'd not seen from her. Watching her interact with her 10B students, I realized that she had only loaned them to me, a gift I still cherish. By the time we decided to leave, we looked like walking snowmen. We found the road and realized we were ten kilometers from the nearest bus stop—and exhausted! Luckily, we were able to hail a rickety bus ambling toward us. Its hunched-over driver opened the door and let us in to its dozen seats and no heat; he charged each of us thirty kopeks. We sat frozen, but our laughing kept us warm as we drove into the city.

As I huddled in my seat, I thought of the closeness of these friends, a warm family beneath the school's formality. They had chosen to be a mini-collective, as if they had declared, "Let's be." It was their own cocoon inside Soviet society made up of cocoons inside cocoons—always as collectives, each cocoon in its own place inside the *matryoshka*. I felt I'd been invited in.

I recalled Zoya Anatolyevna's ninth-form family in Moscow School N° 21. Irina's 10B family was but one part of the tenth form, her mini-family. Such "families" compensated for the coldness of the authorities, enforcers with no concern for the individual. In Irina Dmitrievna's and Zoya Anatolyevna's families, each person counted. Each was respected for who she was.

And I felt respected for who I was. Each time we met, we became closer. We spoke of things that mattered, and ate apples, slid down a snow trail on plastic bags, and laughed on a chilly bus. With them, my role of teacher-as-entertainer could rest. My ego could rest as well. I could be me, and that was enough. Despite lapses since then—and there have been plenty—that self has remained. I sit at my desk writing this. No pretensions. Just me writing.

On my last day, 10B presented me with a light-blue, eight-panel, foldout book. I had received student-made books in Leningrad but none like this. Their black-and-white photos and accompanied writings in colorful magic markers brought tears to my eyes. Their English may not have been perfect, but their thoughts were.

> *I want to tell you that only my thanks to you I have changed myself. I now look at the world with the same eyes but with a changed heart and mind. Our life consists of many interesting things I didn't know before. I was like a nut closed to them. This nut was opened by you. I promise you to find my right road in my life and live with my heart. You helped me to understand the heart of life. You helped me to love it as it is. ~Tanya*

Well, there is one thing I can promise you. I'll never wash the dishes to wash the dishes. I tried once and that was enough! Just for today. ~Ira

Now I can hear and enjoy the music of my soul. I know I'm gonna miss you. I'll never forget our lessons. I hope someday you'll come back like Mary Poppins with the west wind but with the help of Pan Am. Thank you for being so kind, so patient, friendly, and warm to us. ~Maya

You understand not only me, but each of us, each of us as a person. You like us all as we are, Mr. Thoms. You didn't force us to your meditations, ideas, thoughts. You said all that was in your soul. Good luck to you, to all the people you love. Don't worry, be happy. ~Irene

Let's turn all the evil into kindness. ~Irina

Thanks to your lessons, I understand that it is necessary to live just for today. I never thought before that a person has his own choice. And it depends upon a person as to how to live this difficult life. And it is the choice of each of us to choose this or that road. Of course, life is difficult. If you want to live it happy you must respect every person, and maybe you must live just for today. ~Svetlana

I like you, because you like life . . . . I think it is very important after the troubles to say that all the bad was, and before us is only the best. I think that the life is not so difficult, and we must live because God gave us the life . . . . I've thought about my heart, soul, mind, about my future. I have everything we spoke about in my heart. I thought that I would think about it

later, but you forced me to think about it today. Thank you for
all that you are. ~Lena

I HAD BEEN an American teaching in a Party-dominated country in an educational system imposed from Moscow across eleven time zones throughout fifteen Republics. In these last encounters with Soviet students, I'd had the privilege to discuss material far from the traditional curriculum. My students brought their spiritual quests into the classroom. They wrote from their souls, away from the cloak of Communism.

I sensed a longing in these students. I had popped the cork off the bottle of their lives and was empowering them to speak about their deepest concerns. Gone was the prompting, the raising of right hands at the elbow, having to stand to speak, the urge to whisper, the need to cheat, and having to listen to teacher chastisements for being unprepared. We were exploring what was meaningful, touching the spiritual. I had tasted such conversations at Elvira's School N° 185 and at Zoya's School N° 21, but not as deep nor as intense. I would carry these experiences with me into my future teaching, perhaps not in every lesson, but as often as possible.

Before I left, I asked for a letter of recommendation to help me obtain a teaching position when I returned. Rima Ivanovna, principal, and Elena Nikolaevich, head of English combined to write:

To whom it may concern:

Administration, teachers, and students of School No. 15 express their sincere gratitude to Frank Thoms, the teacher from America who worked at our school for 2.5 months and won our hearts completely during this time.

His lessons in all classes, junior and senior, were not usual. There was an atmosphere of understanding and belief

in his lessons. He could create the atmosphere of communi-
cation in the deepest meaning of this word when there is no
barrier, no fear that you won't be understood properly, and
words pass from your soul. His lessons in the primary were so
full of humor, jokes, and games that it was impossible for the
kids to be indifferent . . . .

Frank helped our teachers overcome the language barrier
and helped them understand that they could speak and get
pleasure communicating in English. Not all people have the
gift to communicate. Such people are rare, but these people are
necessary in our society, because they have a sincere interest
in people.

Because Frank has many friends at our school, we hope
that his visit is not his last.

EXCEPT, I ALMOST failed to leave the city.

The school paid me in rubles, enough for spending money and to share expenses with Irina. Rubles, as I saw them, were "Ruble-opoly" money, only good on a Soviet game board. It never occurred to me that I would need dollars.

In late March, after my brother called to say that our mother was failing, I needed to return home. When I applied for a ticket to Leningrad, Aeroflot insisted that I pay $196 (in dollars), about 600 rubles. I had nowhere near that amount of money. To purchase a ticket in rubles, I would need only 150. But as an American I could not use them.

I was unwittingly drawn into the helplessness that many of my friends expressed in dealing with the system: bureaucracies, road-blocks, shortages, frustrations. No one was surprised to learn of my predicament. My friends took action, applying their own form of *blat*—networking under the radar. They purchased a ticket in rubles and made reservations for me to fly to Leningrad. And they procured a Soviet passport, which I solemnly agreed to send back as soon as I arrived. The passport depicted a bald two-hundred-pound-plus, round-faced Russian who bore no resemblance to my skinnier self with wavy, gray-white hair.

And my friend Larissa Ivanova, the tall, energetic sports organizer from the camp, mandated, "Frank, *you cannot utter one Russian word* from the moment you step into the airport! If you do, you will be found out. *Not one word, especially* when you show your passport when changing planes!" Russians, much like the French, are particular about how people enunciate their language. Even if I used my best pronunciation, I would immediately be unmasked. I vowed to keep my mouth shut.

Still, I was sure the KGB would detect my disguise, especially when I changed planes, but I had no choice. When I stepped into the bag-check line, Larissa, who had come to say goodbye, waved frantically from across the lobby, pulled me aside, and whispered, "You *can't* go through that line. They will discover who you really are!" She employed her *blat* yet again and delivered me onto the ramp to the plane without having to pass through security.

And I did not say a word on the five-and-a-half-hour flight. Sitting in the dimly lit Tupolev, I ate dry chicken and drank cold coffee. Each time a flight attendant walked past my seat, I'd drop my eyes. At the stopover, walking into the terminal I kept my head down as I lifted the passport up to the officer sitting in a booth—and when returning to the plane. I tried not to think of what would have happened had I been caught. Arriving in Leningrad near midnight, I was never happier to see my friend Misha Baushev.

BEFORE I LEFT, I hand-wrote a note to 10B and asked Irina to give it to them after I boarded the plane. I may have been writing to me as well.

Give yourselves the gift of inner peace. As you make your choices in life, let your heart prompt you. In your struggles, let them be with love in your heart.

Honor your lives. Don't let anyone fool you that your life is in someone else's hands. Seize your life. Seize the joy despite the sorrows.

I shall never forget you.

Frank

On the plane to Leningrad, I wrote another letter:

I've read the gift of your foldout book and hold you close to my heart. I bless the relationship we have. I am touched deeply by your words, and your love of life.

Life is without a doubt miraculous-a whole series of miracles, moment to moment, miracle to miracle. I know our having met is one of them.

Thank you for touching my life and for trusting yourselves to share your hearts with each other and with me.

Frank

I don't believe that I ever had a closer relationship with students. But it faded as time passed. I wrote twice more, once in May, again in November. I asked them to take special care of Irina Dmitrievna. I now understood how she had willingly given them to me, how she had stepped aside to allow us to form our special relationship. In my last letter, I still yearned somehow to stay close to them. Writing about them has helped.

> *What is for me, your American drop-in, now that I've read-mitted myself into the mainstream of American life? How do you think of me now, so far away, so removed from the life of School N° 15?*
>
> *When I was with you, it was as if I'd always been with you. Now that I am in another school, I know that I'm there for the first time as a beginning. It's not the same as coming to you, not the same.*
>
> *And, it's a wonderful school . . . .*

A couple of weeks later, I received my last letter. It was from Tanya and Luda, whose poem was a fitting conclusion to our correspondence:

> *Everything around is interesting,*
> *Sunrise, moonlight, wind, and waves.*
> *And the troubles are not counting*
> *Because they cannot leave a deep trace.*
> *Never mind! They soon will pass away!*
> *Quiet thoughts and feelings will return.*
> *You'll enjoy your life just for today,*
> *And unusual love in your heart will burn.*

Promises to stay in touch slipped into the ether. There were no more letters. Our lives, more than six thousand miles apart, ventured into new places, new relationships. Busyness became front and center with less and less time to remember what we'd once treasured. Even if I had their addresses, given that the Soviet Union collapsed, street addresses in Alma-Ata (now Almaty) have been changed.

Nearly thirty years later, I am grateful to reflect on my time in Alma-Ata, at the camp and at School N° 15. I was lucky to return to a country I'd come to respect, but on different terms. I often wonder what happened to 10B's Tanya, Olga, Ira, Eduard, Sasha, Lena, Maya, Irene, Irina, Zhenya, Svetlana, Dima, Luda, and Irina Dmitrievna .... who they have become, away from that brief pause we shared near the end of Communism and before the rise of Putin's autocracy. What are they feeling now? What do they believe? What are their hopes? Their fears?

AT THE END of October 1988, my fifth trip, I believed I'd come close to understanding the Russians. I'd slipped into private places inside the *matryoshka*. I'd listened to countless personal stories and discovered idiosyncrasies, notably *shparlgaka, podskazka,* and lying. I began writing my book in earnest to let people know who the Russians were, and how I, an American, was able to thrive in their Communist country.

When I traveled in 1990 to the Pioneer camp in Alma-Ata and returned in January 1991 to teach at School N° 15, I had come under different circumstances. My relationships with Kathleen and Irina became a no-win situation. I'd committed to Kathleen, then had an affair with Irina, then wanted to recommit to Kathleen. Returning to Alma-Ata to Irina's flat felt more a matter of fate than choice.

But by the time I left School N° 15, I'd been drawn into new territory as a teacher. I'd found a space in the *matryoshka* where the separate ways of Russia and America did not exist, where my students and I interfaced on the same plane. I would come home with a new perspective on teaching and on my life. And it was time to ask Kathleen to marry me. I became only more determined to do so when she said she would not marry me unless I found a job. The irony of her demand was that I *did* find a teaching position at a private school, got a *yes* from her—*and* I would again be teaching Russian history to eighth-graders!

I'd come full circle. Six years before, after twenty-five years of teaching about Marx, the Russians, and the Soviet Union, I had stepped on Russian soil for the first time. I returned six more times, primarily to Soviet schools. I would now return to the classroom in a new school to again pursue the Russians. Two weeks before starting my new position, Kathleen and I wed. Once Mikhail Gorbachev resigned, Communism was no more. I'd been fortunate to have experienced his Soviet Union during his nearly seven years in power. A time in Russian history when totalitarianism was put on hold, a time Russians will likely not see again.

WHAT HAPPENS WHEN we step into another culture? As tourists, we taste and leave. But when we choose to plunge in, as I did in my search behind the red veil for the inner dolls of the *matryoshka*, we become changed. We return home and reenter our culture with different perspectives, different ways to commit to our lives. The Russian experiences pushed my envelope. Each trip proved unique. Each demanded a different response. By the time I returned home from teaching at School Nº 15, I was open to a new future. Would I find a teaching position? What kind of school might I become a part of? What kind of teacher would I be? Could I bring my newfound philosophy and the spiritual into my new classroom? And into my life?

I'd always thought that I related to students as people first. In Alma-Ata at the Pioneer camp, my conversation at the ball field with Woo-man rekindled my reflective self. At School Nº 15, I became open to my vulnerability as my students exposed their own vulnerabilities. Despite our defined roles—they as students, I as teacher—we shared a place of mutual respect. Could that happen here? Now that I was in a new school and community, I wanted to be seen as one who cared about others, who was thoughtful, who paid attention to what others needed. And not just as a teacher, but as a colleague, as a community member, and in my new marriage. I committed to a deeper sense of personal integrity and to the importance of retaining it under stress, which would be tested in the coming years.

Would I be as willing to be vulnerable when working under contract? Would I be willing to take risks beyond what would be expected of me? Would students feel comfortable opening their minds and hearts in the way that my Alma-Ata students had?

In Alma-Ata, my personal values had become closer to my teaching values. And this happened in a country whose government demanded followers, not citizens who could think. I discovered invoking spiritual practices inside this paradigm. I was tempted to shout my discovery from the rooftops. Yet teaching is not about preaching. Irene's comment from 10B reminded me of my disposition:

> *You understand not only me, but each of us, each of us as a person. You like us all as we are, Mr. Thoms. You didn't force us to your meditations, ideas, thoughts. You said all that was in your soul.*

POSTSCRIPT
NOT FOR THE MONEY BUT
FOR THE SOUL

In conversations with Alla and others in Yekaterinburg, they reminded me that the individual was persona non grata in the Soviet Union—and now in the new Russia. . . . "There is equality in poverty," a friend put it.

Diary, June 1994

"**F**rank, I would like to invite you to lead a two-week seminar for teachers in Yekaterinburg. You will work with a delegation who will work in schools around New England this fall. We will cover your expenses." Vera Nordal, head of the Boston Area Teachers' Exchange, paused on her phone. "Are you interested?"

Am I interested? Miss another chance to be with Russians—and in a new city! By the end of our conversation we'd nearly finalized plans. The seminar would be in July 1994, during summer break. Kathleen, her son, and I had moved to Massachusetts three years before where I'd accepted an appointment to teach Russian history at a private school. I didn't think I would return to Russia, not because I didn't want to go but because of the cost. When I traveled back to School N° 185 in the spring of 1987, I paid for the trip with much of my savings, which included an international hotel room rate of $135 per night. When I was an exchange teacher, the US government paid.

IT WAS NINE years after my first trip when I again flew into Leningrad's Pulkovo II Airport. Going through passport control was a breeze. Since the fall of Communism three years earlier, Russian officials had become used to foreign travelers and acted less suspicious. It was a different time—and it wasn't. Much was familiar on St. Petersburg streets, except for the billboards: ComputerLand, Sony, Samsung, Coca-Cola . . . and some foreign cars (I thought there'd be more). I walked past the new Grand Europe Hotel rebuilt by the Swedes, slick and elegant, a far cry from the old one. New Intourist buses departed from the entrance in front of its sleek atrium: Finnish-made, clean, brown, sleek, ready to take guests into Intourist's scheduled cocoon.

I sensed a new outer doll, the new-Russia cloak replacing the Soviet cloak. Cloaks within cloaks, the same game, the same duplicity. Each layer covering for the next (I hadn't thought of that before). In the evening, I walked the Summer Gardens with my friend Katya. We walked past my former hotel, the Baltiskaya, now remodeled the Nevsky Palace, remade for the rich, a place for them to feel at home. From new hotel to new hotel in this burgeoning capitalist economy, these rich would never see the Russian culture behind the red veil (yes, it was still there), but only what was presented to them, that polished outer layer of the *matryoshka*.

At the Baltiskaya, I made friends with the housekeepers, the front desk, the waiters. I never met the KGB operative who was to keep an eye on me and my fellow exchange teacher. I wish I had, as I think he would have been a likable guy. After all, he had been protecting my colleague and me. That's how I saw him.

The next day in the late afternoon, I took a metro to Natasha and Slava's apartment on Bolshoi Prospekt in Petrogradskaya. I'd been a couple of times since we first met in 1985. Given our language constraints and different life paths, we had never written to each other. I wanted to see her, though, in part because she had been the first Russian I'd met, and I was curious about her life in the new Russia. When I came this last time, only she and Yuri were in her flat. She looked tired but seemed to lighten up when she saw me. Yuri, who was now twenty, taller, still with his mother's wild curls, appeared listless and made little effort to communicate. I was surprised to learn that her husband, Slava, was gone, by her wish; she indicated (I think) that she hated him. I had thought that they had a good relationship, not full of affection but one more than cordial.

The flat appeared in shambles, as if an earthquake had struck. The kitchen floor was buckling. The hall floor felt squishy, the living room looked like a storage unit, a smelly, tatty mattress curled up in the corner, paint peeling, especially around the windows.

Somehow with our language constraints, we managed to share bits of what had happened in our lives since we had last had seen each other more than six years earlier. She prepared a simple supper that included my favorite pea salad and borscht. Her behavior reminded me of our first lunch. After eating, Yuri went out to see friends. Tired for having walked a lot that day, I lay down on the couch while Natasha left to wash the dishes. I closed my eyes.

As I was thinking I'd overstayed my welcome, I saw Natasha standing before me in a short, revealing black negligee, a sensual Natasha, a sexy Natasha, a Natasha I'd never seen, never imagined. Her wildly curled hair was fluffed more than usual; she flashed a smile, inched closer, committed and confident. Enticing!

"Nyet! Nyet, Natasha!" I couldn't think of any other Russian words. In part from feeling guilty about becoming aroused, I scrambled off the couch, nearly falling, and gestured for her to stay back. I so wanted to explain my feelings, that I was not interested in having sex despite her tempting offer, and to remind her (and me) that I was married. And, surprisingly, I wished that I could let her know that I saw her as a vivacious, courageous person who had risked approaching the American at the airport, who cared for him during his first days in her country, and took him to his first Soviet school.

I began to back away. Still she came on. I stepped toward the door as she lunged toward me showing no inhibition. I grabbed my coat. She became angry, acting as if I were betraying her. I went out the door and practically ran down the smelly concrete stairway, intending to head back to my hotel. Throwing a coat over her negligee, she followed me down the four floors to the street but no further. As I headed toward the Petrogradskaya metro station, looking back to see her standing alone, I felt distraught, wondering how we'd come to this point. We'd met, a wide-eyed American tourist and a brave Russian mother in the airport. Now we parted as a man and a woman in a predicament I had not anticipated. Yet, down deep I had to admit that I felt flattered.

As I walked back to my hotel, I thought about her and worried that she would not survive well in the new Russia. Her husband gone, her children nearly grown, her life perhaps in shambles like her apartment. Yet, she had been the person who dared to come to the airport that October night in 1985, to step in front of me and become my first "real Russian" friend. She had chutzpah. And she had the wherewithal to come on to her American friend with no inhibition.

WALKING THE STREETS the next day, I stopped to buy an ice cream at a kiosk. Five-hundred-fifty rubles! It used to be fifteen kopeks! The dollar–ruble exchange had escalated to two thousand rubles to the dollar, a far cry from the official three-to-one exchange and twenty-to-one on the street that I first encountered in 1985. Then fifteen kopeks equaled about five cents; now 550 rubles equaled about twenty-five cents. I'd heard about inflation in the new Russia. The stores seemed better stocked with fewer lines in the streets.

The Russian people looked much the same. Few colors. Few smiles.

Communism had collapsed; Yeltsin, capitalism, and democracy were on the horizon. But like the ever-elusive "building Communism" under the Party, democracy was destined to receive the same fate. No one seemed willing to predict Russia's future. But the same patterns persisted: daily shopping for kasha, tomatoes, cucumbers, scallions, peas, tea, and potatoes, potatoes, potatoes; women street sweepers, their brooms fashioned with branches; men in tattered, baggy clothes lined up in the morning waiting for beer kiosks to open; the metro, the same price with three zeros added, noisy, smelly as ever, the proverbial *osteratciya, dveri zakryvayutsya*, warning, doors closing, before the doors would slam.

Another friend, Olga from School N° 185, took me to a hospital built for the poor by Catherine the Great. It was still for the poor—and filthy; I saw doctors in dirty white coats. No one was in the hospital's main office, despite it being open hours. Soviet bureaucracy. Olga had her document book—*PCфCP*—to record credits for her third-year pediatric practice. Her only record of her studies; if it were lost, there'd be no documentation. Her situation reminded me of class registers in schools, the only record of students' grades—without the record book, no grades. Once some students tore out pages of their book; the grades were never recovered.

And jazz musicians, whom I first saw in 1991, were playing at the Nevsky Prospekt metro entrance. In my walk with Katya the evening before in the Summer Gardens—quiet, peaceful as ever—she told me about Elvira Nikolaevna's clever connections with budding entrepreneurs to make School N° 185 a favorite in the city. And before returning late to my hotel: the White Nights, eerie, magical, wonderful.

So what had I expected to find, returning to Leningrad? (I know it is now St. Petersburg, but it will always be Leningrad to me.) It had been three years. But time can play tricks on us. Thinking we can reconnect with people and find them the same can be naive. We forget that not only other people change, but we ourselves change.

When returning to a place after having been away for years, we want it to speak to us as it had. We want to find those we care about to be well and happy. We want what was good still to be good. But when we step back and see what was for what it was and leave it there, we can move into the new with open eyes. The challenge of being American in the new Russia meant to take a new approach, to see the new red veil for what it was, and to seek new layers of the *matryoshka*.

SAYING GOODBYE TO friends, I boarded the train at the Moskovsky railway station to begin my thirty-two-hour journey to Yekaterinburg in the Ural Mountains near the border of Europe and Asia. I was apprehensive about being safe, as the protection of Soviet Communist law and order no longer existed. The release of central control—temporary as it was destined to be—caused anxiety for some of my friends and now for me. I was an American on a train, alone with my belongings, an obvious foreigner. An easy target. I stayed as inconspicuous as I could. I recalled my flight from Alma-Ata to Leningrad with a fake passport in April, 1991, the other time I was uncomfortable in what had become my adopted home.

This July train ride unveiled the green countryside that I'd passed on my way back to Alma-Ata, that snowy January of 1991. At Perm station—where Aleksandr Solzhenitsyn lived—disrepair reared its ugly presence. From my train window, I saw tattered wood poles on each end of a soccer pitch, grassless with large worn spots. Peasants—dirty, in tattered clothes, sleeping on large bundles—and passed-out drunks, all waiting for trains. Four telephone booths, two defunct, handsets missing. Taxis in line waited. Two well-heeled mothers, clean and smartly dressed, strolled past with three children. A main street sign, Ulitza Lenin. And, surprise, some beautiful gardens!

Yekaterinburg looked as I'd expected, a former Soviet city with the similar accouterments of Leningrad, Moscow, and Kiev: aluminum-framed kiosks, cement buildings, state stores, old buses, and now American films in theaters—no titles I recognized—foreign-ad billboards, and the ubiquitous Russian Lada Zhiguli cars, few black Volgas, and even fewer foreign cars.

I held my first seminar with the Russians who were to come to New England, a dozen curious, interested educators eager to learn about America. I'd been warmly invited to come to Yekaterinburg, but these teachers told me how jealous their directors and colleagues were of them, because they were going to the States. Securing permission to leave the country was difficult; even seeking permission to travel within was a challenge.

Overall, our seminars happened as if I were teaching at home. We met for three weeks, six hours a day exploring survival English, the culture of the Boston area, and educational practices in the US. We went to sites in the city, including museums and government buildings. As was my modus operandi, I became integral with them in the seminar rather than a teacher-in-the-rye hoping to rescue them.

Alla Nagovitsina was the leader, witty and charming, the most savvy, the most skilled in English. She guided the discussions, offered provocative ideas, and encouraged the others. She let me into her life, into her struggles with bureaucracies, and reminded me that what had been "Soviet" was still in place. The KGB—abolished in October 1991 by Gorbachev became the FSB—still wielded power. *Bumaga*, the proverbial bureaucratic paperwork, still ruled. To curry favor for her school, Alla wielded boxes of chocolates to bribe officials as thank-yous to lay the groundwork for the next time.

These teachers were eager to know about the US education system, similar to my hunger for theirs. They were eager to please, again something I've felt from other Russian teachers. But in our conversations, they revealed the Russian sense of inferiority in comparison to the West, something that came to light during Gorbachev. Before Gorbachev, Russians were led to believe that they lived on a par with the rest of the developed world.

Feeling inferior can be painful. Whenever this feeling emerges, a person may choose to repress it. Russians who might have sought to come out from under this feeling, from this repressed way of life, tended to band together to maintain their inferior circumstances. They would shun others who were attempting to raise their standards, their position in life. It was another manifestation of the deeply embedded Russian collective mindset.

THE LANDSCAPE AROUND the city looked like a war zone, a plethora of dirt and dust and rutted roads. Ludmilla, one of the teachers, recounted with a sigh that "on these roads, you try to get there or try to get out if you can." And unkempt pathways were evident between the clustered nondescript high-rises. Common property was disrespected, the litter less than in the US only because there was less to litter. Stairwells resembled the paint-peeling, urine-infested one at Natasha's flat on Bolshoi Prospekt in Leningrad. Yet locks and codes were plentiful at front entrances, ostensibly to protect private property inside—what little there was.

Again Russians were hesitant to offer invitations to the American, to flats not good enough in their minds. Yet when visits were arranged, the warmth and hospitality was the same, the food delicious, the vodka and cognac more than fine. Once I went to a village where two of the teachers were preparing to meet the American. On a bumpy bus ride, flinging dust in our wake, we arrived at Tatyana and Victor's "mansion," complete with good food and a *banya*, in a village with its own sports palace. And their farm implements included an antique sickle forged in the late nineteenth century at this country home of two teachers about to come to America.

During our conversation, Alla reinforced much of what I've come to understand about the Russians.

"Why," I asked her, "is Russian literature so prominent in your culture?"

"It's morose, it has deep sadness. The characters doing what they're told, a hesitancy to commit crimes. Who is a free man? He does what he's told, and he does what the group does. And oh, the double meanings: Russians always speak this way." Alla drew a breath, "A classic example is of a woman preparing a dinner who says, 'I've just thrown this together quickly for you.' Never, never is this the case!"

Her words reminded me of Pavel Kozhevnikov's image of the knight on the chessboard, where we think one way, say another, and do the third. Oh, the Russian penchant for ambiguity.

Later, when Alla's friends, Vera and Volodya, had returned from an afternoon outing, Alla told me that Volodya took a nap while Vera arranged for his train ticket to Moscow—a difficult process. And Vera procured the food and arranged for their special trip to the lake region—all without a telephone and a car.

"Women work, men talk," Alla said.

And later in that conversation, she added, "Russians feel hesitant to meet foreigners. A case in point, Frank, Irina's husband did not show up for our goodbye dinner, as he was 'embarrassed,' 'afraid to be there.'"

Another example of the pain of feeling inferior. It may have originated during the Golden Horde occupation of Russia for nearly three centuries. While Europeans were having a Renaissance exploring science, religion, the arts and humanities, Russians were paying tribute to the Mongols. This subjugation forced them to stay close for survival and to turn away from Europe. No means to break out, to experiment, to consider alternatives. Stay together, be together. Then they would survive.

Alla arranged a visit to a turbine factory. As we walked in, we could see that OSHA would have been appalled. A huge unwieldy space, rubble everywhere, parts crammed in open bins, metal shavings scattered, unguarded holes waiting to lacerate a leg, cranes dangling objects overhead; dank air, leaking roofs, buckets collecting water; and workers lingering about. What would this place be like in winter? I wondered.

Alla introduced me to Ivan, the supervisor and her friend. Short, plump, in a gray disheveled suit with balding hair, he invited us into his office to sit at a table perpendicular to his mammoth desk, Lenin's picture under broken glass behind his chair, four telephones (one direct to Moscow no longer working), and vodka for guests—a similar arrangement to director Rima Alexandrovna's cabinet at School N° 169. He gestured to invite us to take a tour. I felt his shame as he explained the factory's glorious days with three shifts building turbines from scratch—now a fragment of what it was. At sixty-two and with declining eyesight, he was ready to retire.

Ivan's deteriorating factory was yet another example of the failed Soviet Union.

AFTER THE SEMINAR, Alla invited me to travel to her grandmother's home in Izhevsk, a half day by train from Yekaterinburg, and a day from St. Petersburg. It was in the country, a vast space I'd only imagined from maps. In our short stay, we visited a collective farm—at least we were able to come close. As we approached, seven children suddenly appeared across a slung plank bridge over a river. They were about three to thirteen years old, thin, small, dark-haired, and poorly dressed. Meeting their first foreigner, their eyes widened. We mingled, interacted without language, and hugged before we separated. I found it hard to leave; I wanted to learn more about their lives.

Alla took me to a *Khokhloma* factory where the famous Russian-painted, lustrous, black-based, yellow and red wood-ware was made. We met Tatiana, a long-time employee in her blue shirtdress and white apron, her metal teeth gleaming. She described her craft in broken English and told me about the hardships of her life. Tearing up, she wanted to know why Americans could drive cars while she could not make enough money to take her kids to school.

She expressed pride in her work as she demonstrated her craft on old lathes. She flicked yellow from berries in a bowl with a brush onto a wood spoon. I couldn't help noticing the toxic fumes from the glazing furnace, which she breathed every day; worse in the winter, she told us, as the windows had to be nearly closed. The shop was far more polluted than the exhaust on the streets of Leningrad. We stayed for a while and talked, laughed, and commiserated.

"Do you like what you are painting, layer upon layer, layer upon layer?" I asked with Alla's help.

"Yes," Tatiana replied, "but it's not for the money, it's for the soul." I bought one of her circular cylinders (for soup) with a mini-bowl on top (for salt) and four vessels for drinking. Alla took our picture. I still cherish her beautiful pieces.

Tatiana's claim that her work was "for the soul" reflected the internal Russian, often hidden from outsiders. She was speaking to the inner psyche of those whose integrity supersedes the outer phases of their lives. Where the personal—the self, family, friends—is central to their thoughts and actions. Where who they are is more important than how others perceive them.

The ruble, necessary for sustenance, was not central to their lives. Conversations at the dinner table centered on family, friendship, and sometimes politics, especially during the Gorbachev years. Despite Tatiana's expressed resentment of Americans who could buy what she couldn't, she cared first about herself, her kids, her place in her work, and perhaps her place in the cosmos.

CONVERSATIONS WITH ALLA and others in Yekaterinburg reminded me that the individual had been persona non grata in the Soviet Union—and was still now in the new Russia. Everyone in Leningrad, Moscow, Alma-Ata, and Yekaterinburg had access to the same produce. The flats had the same dark-veneered furniture, small white refrigerators, and four-burner stoves, the same faucets, faux-oriental-patterned rugs on walls, red couches by day that were beds at night. "There is equality in poverty," a friend put it.

Hot water would come when central authorities let it flow; people left it on all day. No need to worry, no need to conserve, to restrict showers. The water would come to them. As the State came to them. No need to choose. Everything was uncomfortable: the metro escalator's handrails in Leningrad and Moscow, which moved faster than you; tired, tilting, overcrowded buses; long lines at shops; difficult access to telephones; offices closed during business hours; and *bumaga*, layers of paperwork, necessary for everything. The State restricted internal passports. The individual did not count.

The West purports to value each person's contributions to society. People are encouraged to take initiative, to explore, invent, create. But when people believe they have no recourse to contribute to the quality of life of society, they withdraw and struggle to maintain their existence. If one risks taking initiative, he will most likely be met with rejection, not only from those in authority but also from his comrades.

In fact, the individual had not counted in Russia for six hundred years under tsarist rule. After the expulsion of the Mongols, Russians peasants were impelled to survive tsarist oppression. In the seventeenth century, the nobility forced peasants to live under serfdom, which meant they were not free and, like slaves, they could be sold but with the land they lived on. Only in the mid-nineteenth century did Alexander II sign a decree eliminating serfdom. But by then, the collective mindset was so deep that most Russians never considered taking initiative to make their lives better.

And suffering was embedded, which I'd felt on that hot, dry summer day, that 330-kilometer Chimkent bus trip. Everyday

frustration and depravity. Russian life meant to endure: work to pro-
cure food, seek bureaucrat approval, struggle to find a flat, endeavor
to make travel arrangements. And having to live with unpredictable
buses whose routes changed without notice, drivers who changed
their minds, and who would pack in twenty extra passengers—dirty,
smelly buses tilted even when empty. Tired buses. Tired Russians.

Taking a walk one morning from Alla's mother's home, I zig-
zagged to avoid puddles. When the sun came out, the puddles became
mud. There was no drainage. Cleaning up was not possible. In winter,
drainpipes spilled on sidewalks, creating ice ridges that lurked below
the snow cover. Everybody knew but could not pay enough attention.
To go from A to B, you picked your way, a friend told me, whether
in the city or in the country, summer or winter. I saw a *bábushka*
carrying two bags go flying in the mud, her feet way out front. She got
up, realigned her shirtdress, repacked her bags, and walked on. Life
in a culture without care. Fate.

I saw another woman passed out, an apparent drunk dragging
her; her young son—maybe ten years old—followed holding her feet.
I stood still not knowing what to do. Another man lurched passed; I
discovered from kids playing nearby, listening with my fragmented
Russian, that such incidents happened a lot.

Drunks symbolized the small world of working-class Russians.
Responding to the stresses of everyday life meant one's focus needed
to be on the present, on getting through the day, the week, the season.
No time to think about what might be, what the future would bring.
Making it to tomorrow was the goal. The drunks reflected total resig-
nation. Nothing was possible, nothing.

Yekaterinburg manifested urban sprawl Russian style. Bland
concrete high-rises engulfed peasant *izbas,* simple log houses, and
swallowed up villages. An old woman collected water from a well
next to a high-rise. The well was for the people who lived in the *izbas.*
They had no water, no toilets. Cows roamed between the high-rises.

Village life, so deep in Russian history, lived on. And inside high-rises, toilets smelled like outhouses left behind. And interspersed were random lines of rusted-metal garages, blights on the landscape.

Despite the increase of available publications from the West since the fall of Communism, myths about America persisted. A woman touched me and swooned; a man stepped off a bus, flipped me the bird, and mumbled, "America your funeral," or something like that. I felt like an object, not a person; an "American" object. Children, on the other hand, delighted in the American despite the lack of common language; they were looking at me, not seeing a foreigner but a person. What are their dreams? I wondered. What do they want to know? What will they come to know about America? And what has become of them?

To FLY HOME I took the train from the Finland Station to Helsinki, my two large black duffle bags full of memorabilia. A Russian in a dark-blue suit sat across from me. Speaking perfect English, he inquired about my trip. I answered without suspicion, naive probably, not wondering whether he might have been KGB. He continued to talk—a lot. As I showed him the contents of one of my suitcases, I figured out who he was. Nothing transpired. He departed in "friendship."

I arrived home on TWA; my two black bags did not. Despite several weeks of inquiring, I never saw them again.

CODA

Why bother to write about a society that collapsed more than twenty-five years ago? Why am I telling you this? And why should you care?

Thirty years ago, I began writing about my time as a teacher behind the red veil, seeking to know Russians in what were to be the last days of the Soviet Union. I intended to explore the culture of "the enemy." I wanted to find common ground and not be the know-it-all American. In schools, teachers and children embraced my humor, my quirky ways, my desire to know everyone's name, and my struggle with their pedagogical habits. On the street and in flats, I heard poignant stories. Some bared their souls.

In every school, every child (almost) wore a uniform, sat in pairs at tables, raised their right hands at the elbow, stood to recite, and with the teacher's permission sat down, folded their arms, palms flat. Everyone succumbed to the national curriculum; every child could recite Pushkin. I began teaching in Leningrad and Moscow from Soviet English-language texts to children seven to seventeen and ended in Alma-Ata discussing the afterlife and reincarnation with sixteen-year-olds.

My experiences in each of the three cities had its own essence. Unwittingly, I may have been an Aladdin who released each child's genie, a longing to break out of a restrictive system. Younger students' right elbows flew off the desks seeking to be recognized. Older students' responses to provocative questions pushed them into unfamiliar territory, mirroring the urgency of Soviets wanting to break-out of a tired, oppressive system.

Upon reflection, I was the primary beneficiary of my sojourns. As I probed the *matryoshka* in befriending Russians, I was befriending me. And the more vulnerable I became, the more we could connect. I was a foreigner—an American at that—who wanted to understand the Russians. In the process, I became more willing to evoke the heart and the spiritual in the classroom and in my life. Underlying my relationships was a search for meaning, for what mattered. My effort to probe Churchill's "Russia is a riddle wrapped in a mystery inside an enigma" became a process of self-deciphering. I have the Russian people to thank.

Throughout this book you've seen Russians struggling to make life work, improvising to meet needs, expressing a willingness to befriend. Having stayed in touch with some, I see them now as people with the same hopes and dreams. We connected inside Gorbachev's thaw. Elvira Nikolaevna, Irina Nikolaevna, and Raisa Vladimirovna have died. Some have scattered throughout the world. And many are now living under Putin's autocracy.

The Russians I met understood their lives were destined to be inside a unitary state. Nothing was for them. Nothing for the individual. To live meant to endure. The State, after all, came to them. Trust was not a factor. Mikhail Gorbachev, by opening his country to foreigners, wanted his people to see themselves anew, to hope for a better, less restrictive society. But nearly seven years was not enough time. As of 2019, Vladimir Putin has been elected to his fourth six-year term, sometimes holding an 80 percent plurality. The Russian people have been reassured. They now have, in Svetlana Alexievich's wise words, "our collective Putin." [2] And Putin's *pokazukha*: a nuclear-powered Russia with an economy trailing behind Canada's but an ideology equal to the West.

The Gorbachev thaw lasted nearly seven years, my years mingling with Russians. In *Behind the Red Veil: An American inside Gorbachev's Russia,* you've ventured alongside this American who has told his story of seeking out the Russian people everywhere he could—and seeking to know himself in the process.

My relationships with Russians became unwritten contracts in which each of us trusted the other to speak honestly in our encounters. And the more I came to know them, the more I fell in love with them, even those with whom I had a falling-out. I have taken the responsibility to write compassionately, because they opened their hearts and minds countless times in countless circumstances. And they opened mine.

NOTES

Chapter XI

1. Scott Peck, *The Road Less Traveled: A New Psychology of Love, Traditional Values and Spiritual Growth* (New York: Touchstone, 1978), 15.

Coda

2. David Remnick, *The New Yorker Radio Hour*, March 16, 2018.

ACKNOWLEDGMENTS

A teacher-turned-writer stands first on his remarkable students: from Hanover, New Hampshire's junior–senior high and middle schools and Bancroft School's middle school in Worcester, Massachusetts. These students let me explore multiple entry points into Marxism, Russian history, and Soviet Communism. In my eight trips to the Soviet Union and the new Russia, I taught countless students in Leningrad Schools N° 185 and N° 169; in Moscow School N° 21; and in Alma-Ata (now Almaty), Kazakhstan, School N° 15. These students taught me more than they realized.

To Del Goodwin, my first mentor, who opened the door to propagating my penchant for the Russians. To Pat Davenport, who had the wisdom to support my two-week leave from the classroom for my first trip. To Elvira Nikolaevna, Irina Nikolaevna, Raisa Vladimovna, Zoya Anatolyevna, Elena Vladimovna, Irina Dmitrievna, Victoria Sadovskaya, Misha Baushev, Valentina Vladimirovna, and their Soviet colleagues who took this American into their confidence.

To G-G Tritschler, head of Bancroft, who invited me to teach

Russian history to its eighth-graders where I could share my new understandings of the Russian people.

To people who've supported my writing efforts for the past fifteen years: Susan Page, Dinty Moore, Gerald Helferich, Jenn David-Lange, Ursula Boyle, Hugh Silbaugh, Rob Fried, John D'Auria, Sam Intrator, Bob Milley, Vincent Rogers, Joyce Barnes, Janis Owens, Paul Reville, Pamela Penna, Parker Palmer, Rebecca Langrall, Mona Seno, Eric Waite, Carolyn Pool, Anne Wheelock, Ben Klompus, Joanne Henessey, Diane Dugas, Linda Ellis, Gale Berry, Donna Talman, Ron Stegall, Peter Bien, Barnes Boffey, Kate Gagnon, Liz Morantz, Melissa Matta, Tom Payzant, Susan Engel, Page Tomkins, Tony Polito, Victoria Robbins, Jill Mirman, Alex Ruthman, Bill Murphy, and Ford Daley.

To Chet Kozlowski, whose writing sessions invited valuable commentaries from him and Ken Morrow, Linda Laino, Lynn Learned, Tasha Paley, Cami Sands, and Sharon Steeber, all of whom helped frame this book. And to David Ramsey and Diana Spechler whose intensive writing workshops were invaluable.

To the inimitable and ever supportive April Eberhardt, my wondrous agent. To Brooke Warner and Lauren Wise of Spark Press whose wisdom shepherded me to publication. To Annie Tucker whose inestimable editing skills brought life to the book—a gift to this writer and to his readers. To Elisabeth Kauffman whose penchant for detail made the manuscript better. To Julie Metz for the book's radiant cover. And to Sid Balman Jr., who offered me valuable advice.

A special tribute to my first editor, Christina Ward, formerly of Little Brown, who died shortly after shepherding me through my first book. Her confidence launched me into becoming a serious writer.

And to Kathleen Cammarata, my wife and friend, who offered endless insights and support. Her critiques opened the door to more honest writing about the Russians and about me.

ABOUT THE AUTHOR

After twenty-five years in the classroom teaching Marxism, Russian History, and Soviet Communism, Frank Thoms traveled behind the Iron Curtain for the first time in October 1985. After seven more trips, the last being three years after the fall of Gorbachev and Communism, he decided to write about his insights into the Russian people—and his insights into himself.

From his first moments, he was able to slip behind the red veil: the face of Communism that the Soviet Union projected onto its own citizens, foreign visitors, and the world at large. From his first tour, where he met a Russian mother and her two children at the airport in Leningrad, he ventured his way into places he may not have belonged.

Once he tasted meeting Russians behind the red veil, he found his way to return as a teacher in four Soviet schools in three cities: Leningrad, Moscow, and Alma-Ata, Kazakhstan. Twice he was selected to be a US–Soviet exchange teacher, and twice he ventured there to teach in schools on his own. His detailed accounts of these encounters offer an inside look at the Russians, their thoughts, feelings, hopes, and fears. In the process he discovered much about himself. Given the relaxation of governmental pressure during Gorbachev's reign, Frank engaged in countless open discussions.

He looked for common ground to connect with Russians, not to judge but to learn, not to bring America to them, but to be an American with them.

The Journalist: Life and Loss in America's Secret War, Jerry A. Rose and Lucy Rose Fischer $16.95, 978-1-68463-065-3
A collaboration between Lucy Rose Fischer and her late brother, *The Journalist* tells the story of Jerry Rose, a young journalist and photographer who exposed the secret beginnings of America's Vietnam War in the early 1960s. He interviewed Vietnamese villagers, embedded himself with soldiers, and wrote the first major article about American troops fighting in Vietnam.

*The Restless Hungarian: Modernism, Madness, and The American Dream,*Tom Weidlinger $16.95, 978-1-943006-96-0
A revolutionary, a genius, and a haunted man . . . The story of the architect-engineer Paul Weidlinger, whose colleagues called him "The Wizard," spans the rise of modern architecture, the Holocaust, and the Cold War. The revelation of hidden Jewish identity propels the author to trace his father's life and adventures across three continents.

Mission Afghanistan: An Army Doctor's Memoir, Elie Cohen, translation by Jessica Levine $16.95, 978-1-943006-65-6
Decades after evading conscription as a young man, Franco-British doctor Elie Paul Cohen is offered a deal by the French Army: he can settle his accounts by becoming a military doctor and serving at Camp Bastion in Afghanistan.

Engineering a Life: A Memoir, Krishan K. Bedi $16.95, 978-1-943006-43-4
A memoir of Krishan Bedi's experiences as a young Indian man in the South in the 1960s, this is a story of one man's perseverance and determination to create the life he'd always dreamed for himself and his family, despite his options seeming anything but limitless.

About SparkPress

SparkPress is an independent, hybrid imprint focused on merging the best of the traditional publishing model with new and innovative strategies. We deliver high-quality, entertaining, and engaging content that enhances readers' lives. We are proud to bring to market a list of *New York Times* best-selling, award-winning, and debut authors who represent a wide array of genres, as well as our established, industry-wide reputation for creative, results-driven success in working with authors. SparkPress, a BookSparks imprint, is a division of SparkPoint Studio LLC.

Learn more at GoSparkPress.com